D0604570

Discovering Matthew

THE GUIDEPOSTS HOME BIBLE STUDY PROGRAM

Floyd W. Thatcher   *General Editor*
Robin White Goode   *Associate Editor*
Bob E. Patterson   *Technical Consultant*

EDITORIAL ADVISORY BOARD

Lloyd J. Ogilvie
Senior Minister, First Presbyterian Church
of Hollywood

David A. Hubbard
President, Fuller Theological Seminary

Charles L. Allen
Senior Minister Emeritus, First United
Methodist Church of Houston

Ruth Stafford Peale
President, Foundation for Christian Living;
Vice President, American Bible Society

Myron S. Augsburger
Pastor, Washington Community
Fellowship Church—Mennonite Church

David L. McKenna
President, Asbury Theological Seminary

Russell H. Dilday, Jr.
President, Southwestern Baptist
Theological Seminary

MATTHEW: THE FIRST GOSPEL

Discovering Matthew	Bob E. Patterson
What This Scripture Means to Me	Elizabeth Rockwood
Photographs	Bruce C. Cresson
Maps	Janice Gibson
Book Design	Elizabeth Woll
Cover Artist	Ben Wohlberg

DISCOVERING MATTHEW

The Guideposts
Home Bible Study Program

GUIDEPOSTS

Carmel   New York 10512

THE GUIDEPOSTS HOME BIBLE STUDY PROGRAM
Matthew: The First Gospel:
     1. DISCOVERING MATTHEW
     2. My Working Bible
     3. Knowing More About Matthew

COPYRIGHT © 1985 by GUIDEPOSTS ASSOCIATES, INC.
     Carmel, N.Y. 10512

All rights reserved. No part of this program or publications within this program, may be reproduced, stored in a retrieval system, or transmitted in any form by any means, electronic, mechanical, photocopying, recording or otherwise, without the written permission of the publisher, Guideposts Associates, Inc., Carmel, New York 10512.

All Scripture verses referenced herein are from the King James Version of the Bible.

Designed by Elizabeth Woll.

Printed in the United States of America.

Contents

Publisher's Introduction

"The Gospels are the Magna Charta of the human spirit," wrote Dr. E. V. Rieu in the Introduction to his superb translation.

History has failed to dim the impact and influence of these magnificent and awesome freedom documents. In them we confront the Central Figure of human history—Jesus of Nazareth. We celebrate His arrival in Bethlehem, learn a little of His early years, and are soon thrust into the realities of an adult Jesus whom we first see striding to the banks of the Jordan to be baptized, moving on quietly to His lonely experience of testing in the Wilderness of Judea, and then entering into His intensely active and consuming ministry of some three and one-half years. His was a ministry of involvement with the needs and hurts of people caught up in trying to carve out a life of meaning and hope.

And so by careful design we turn our attention first in the Guideposts Home Bible Study Program to a thoughtful study of the four Gospels—Matthew, Mark, Luke, and John. Together we will walk in the footsteps of Jesus. We will see and begin to feel something of the tremendous power that was unleashed in our world through His words and actions. It was a power that brought healing to tormented bodies, wholeness to the emotionally disturbed, food to the hungry, and life to the physically and spiritually dead. We will witness the great significance of

Jesus' resurrection and glory in His power over sin and the grave. But more than that, we will better understand how His resurrection power refreshes and restores our lives today, and liberates us to live changed, new lives. It is a power that has changed the course of history from then until now.

Each of the four Gospel writers was uniquely different. Each wrote from a different perspective and out of his own experience. Each one wrote in his own style and with a specific emphasis and audience in mind. But throughout the four Gospels the central figure is always Jesus Christ. We are not involved in reading biography but in meeting a Person.

Similarly, the writers of these lessons on each of the four Gospels are uniquely different, but each is highly competent and thoroughly committed to the Word of God. It is their purpose to capture the drama and the meaning of the Gospel events and message for today in a simple and forthright way. To study under their guidance is an adventure that will help us understand more clearly the depth and meaning of our faith.

We welcome you to this first unit in the Guideposts Home Bible Study Program—the Gospel of Matthew. It is divided into eight lessons, each designed to illuminate with simple clarity its life-changing truth. In each lesson we are taken into the scene and setting of the events in a way that makes them come alive.

We attempted to make the lessons similar in length, but of necessity the lesson on the Sermon on the Mount—Matthew 5 through 7—is longer than most.

The message of the Gospel of Matthew, as we see Jesus through the writer's eyes, is unique to the mood and lifestyle of our times in many ways. To understand this message and its relevance to us is to move forward to an exciting adventure of faith that will enrich and deepen our spiritual lives, and help us in becoming more effective Christians.

Preface

Matthew, Mark, Luke, and John are the most important books in the world because they are our only sources for the life and teachings of Jesus.

Throughout much of church history, many considered Matthew the most popular of the four Gospels. There are several reasons for this popularity, but for our study I'll mention three: **1.** Early tradition said the apostle Matthew wrote it. This has given the Gospel the prestige of an eyewitness account; **2.** It has proven to be an especially effective manual of instruction (particularly for new converts) for use in the church; **3.** The early church included persons of widely divergent opinions and backgrounds who were attracted by the universal spirit found in this "representative Gospel."

The Period of the Unwritten Good News

The Gospel, or the "good news," is that God's age-long purpose for our salvation (revealed first in the Old Testament) has been fulfilled in Jesus the Christ. This truth had been confirmed to the first Christians when Jesus rose from the dead, and by the gift of new life through the Holy Spirit. This "good news" was first recorded on the hearts of the early Christians, and only later was it put into written form.

It may seem strange to us, but the Christians after Pentecost (Acts 2), did not immediately put in writing a definitive biography of Jesus. They didn't feel the need to write one because they expected the Lord to return shortly, and besides, the eyewitnesses of Jesus' life and ministry were there among them.

Who Wrote the Gospel of Matthew: When and Why

Most modern scholars, although they see a connection between this Gospel and the Apostle Matthew, question whether the Gospel as it stands came entirely from the hand of Matthew. It is probable that Matthew was one of the contributors to the Gospel—that is, he compiled a document which became a main source of the Gospel.

When was the Gospel of Matthew written?

After A.D. 70 (Jerusalem had already been destroyed by the Romans) and before A.D. 96 (Clement of Rome apparently knew this Gospel). A.D. 85 is perhaps the best date.

Why was the Gospel of Matthew written?

The Jewish nation was destroyed in A.D. 70 because it had revolted against Rome, but the religion of Judaism survived under the leadership of the Pharisees. At an "academy" in the town of Jamnia near the Mediterranean coast, rabbinic Judaism pulled itself together by excommunicating Christians and strictly interpreting the Old Testament Law. The Gospel of Matthew is an answer to the form of Judaism that came out of Jamnia.

After A.D. 70 both Judaism and Jewish Christianity had to strike a new course. Matthew wrote about these new identities by taking up many issues that were of concern to the rabbis of Jamnia. Matthew openly affirmed the authority of Jesus' teachings over the teachings of the synagogue. He avoided Pharisaic legalism, yet maintained the value of the Law (unlike the libertine gentile Christians who abandoned the Law).

An Outline of the Gospel of Matthew

There are five distinct teaching sections in Matthew. A Narrative section precedes and introduces each Teaching section. A formula that prepares us for a major new block of material concludes each section. Many readers of this Gospel have inferred from this arrangement that Matthew's plan was to construct a new "five books of Moses," a kind of Law of Christ to fulfill the Law of Moses. This has been my approach to outlining Matthew.

The Gospel of Matthew followed the framework of Mark for the account of Jesus' ministry. A short synopsis of the contents may be helpful.

PREAMBLE: The genealogy and birth of Jesus, chapters 1–2.

BOOK I: Concerning discipleship, chapters 3–7.

BOOK II: Concerning apostleship, chapters 8–10.

BOOK III: Concerning revelation and rejection, chapters 11–13.

BOOK IV: Concerning life in the church community, chapters 14–18.

BOOK V: Concerning judgment, chapters 19–25.

EPILOGUE: Jesus' death and resurrection, chapters 26–28.

Whatever outline we choose to follow, the cardinal idea of Matthew is that Jesus is the Christ (Messiah), the Son of God. Jesus came not to destroy the Law of Moses but to fulfill it and to teach us a more excellent way of life as members of a new community, the Christian church.

Characteristics of the Gospel of Matthew

Matthew gives us five discourses. This Gospel's most striking characteristic is its systematic grouping of Jesus' sayings. The main body of Matthew is composed of five great discourses of Jesus' teaching preceded by narratives skillfully adjusted to introduce them. These discourses are: The Sermon on the Mount (5:1–7:29); The Mission Charge to the Twelve (9:35–11:1); Parables on the Mystery of the Kingdom (13:1–52); Life in the Christian Community (18:1–35); and The Drama of the End of the Age (24:1–26:1).

Another characteristic of the Gospel is the explicit fulfillment of Old Testament prophecy by the advent of the Messiah. "All this was done that it might be fulfilled, which was spoken of the Lord by the prophet, saying..." is a theme repeated again and again. Jesus came to fulfill the Old Testament ("...came not to destroy but to fulfill the Law and the Prophets").

When Matthew was writing his Gospel, Jerusalem was in ashes; Rome's grip on the Jews grew tighter, the church was separated from the synagogue, and the rabbis and Pharisees at Jamnia were attempting to rebuild the faith of the Jews around the Law as they interpreted it. Matthew loved the Law; he loved his fellow Jews; and he loved Christ. He wanted to bring the three together in a happy harmony.

DISCOVERING MATTHEW

Matthew's Gospel was written with the needs of the young church in view. Of the four Gospels, Matthew alone mentions the word "church" (*ecclesia*, 16:18; 18:17). He was not interested in the church as an institution, but as a functioning community. In this Gospel, Jesus is bound to the church in covenant just as the God of the Old Testament was bound to Israel; Jesus' disciples signify the qualities of Christian existence, and Simon Peter is both a representative disciple and a symbol of church leaders.

A further word.

As we study, it will be helpful to think of ourselves as one of the disciples of Jesus. Within this group of twelve our identity will shift possibly to Peter, Judas, and Matthew in turn. It will be with Peter, though, that we as modern Christian readers will probably identify ourselves—a wave being made into a rock. We will see in this wavering fisherman much that is akin to our own lives, and in Peter's growing strength under the Master's direction we will find our own hope of strength.

LESSON 1
MATTHEW 1–4

The Birth of Jesus and the Beginning of His Ministry

Lord, Help me to understand this lesson. AMEN.

Most people are somewhat curious about their ancestry, but it took writer Alex Haley in his book *Roots* to reawaken thousands and possibly millions of people to the potential drama in our individual histories. All of us are heavily influenced by both our family history and our geographical background. In many ways our sense of self-worth emerges from an awareness of who we are and where we came from.

Family roots was certainly a factor to Matthew as he began his Gospel and the story of Jesus. With great care he documented Jesus' ancestry through forty-two generations, all the way back to Abraham, the father of the Jewish people.

This was important because in first century Palestine, the Jews, under the cruel and oppressive rule of Rome, were eagerly awaiting the coming of their Messiah. Quite naturally the Messiah had to have the proper heritage. To prove that Jesus had Messianic credentials Matthew traced his lineage through David to Abraham. Further, he knew this record of Jesus' ancestry was especially important to his readers because the rabbis at Jamnia (mentioned in the Preface) were putting together a new form of Ju-

The Genealogy and Birth of Jesus

The importance of Jesus' ancestry.

13

daism that demanded an uncorrupted lineage for every orthodox Jew.

Matthew lists Jesus' human ancestors in three sections of fourteen generations each. From Abraham to David (1:2–6) Israel was welded into a great nation. From David to the exile in Babylon (1:6–11) Israel lost her greatness while the prophets preached both judgment and hope. From the exile to Jesus Christ (1:12–17) God brought His salvation to focus in the Incarnation of His Son and Israel had the chance to regain her greatness. This was Matthew's way of associating Jesus with the three great stages of Israel's history and the salvation story.

But Matthew had a unique sense of irony, a knack of presenting the unexpected and shocking, and a way of refuting the new Judaism emerging from Jamnia. Even in the genealogy he departs from the customary and gives his readers a surprise. It was not traditional to put the names of women in Jewish pedigrees because women didn't have legal rights. But Matthew gives prominence to four women: Tamar, Rahab, Ruth, and Bathsheba. It is interesting to note that all four were gentiles and three of them were suspected of adultery. Matthew seems to be saying that if these scandals lie in the Messiah's background, then God may be more gracious than Israel imagined, and He would shatter all of the preconceived ideas about the Messiah.

Self-righteous Pharisees would be uncomfortable with Jesus' family tree and uneasy in His presence. If Jesus did not come from racially pure stock, then the church community which He founded could not restrict its membership to the race of the Jews. Consequently, this Gospel opens the door for the gentiles and pictures Jesus as the universal Christ.

The Divine heritage.

In chapter one, verses 18–25, Matthew tells the story of Jesus' birth in a simple and beautiful way, but he makes it clear that it took place by the action of the Holy Spirit.

There were three steps to a Jewish marriage: engagement, betrothal, and the ceremony proper. Joseph and Mary were in the one year betrothal period in which they belonged to each other but did not live together as husband and wife. It was during this time that Mary told him she was pregnant by a miraculous act of God. Joseph was a God-fearing man who cared deeply for Mary, but with the news of her pregnancy he agonized over how he could end the betrothal without causing her embarrassment. According to custom a betrothal could only be ended by a public divorce. However, we read that an angel of the Lord appeared to Joseph in a dream with a reassuring message that Mary's baby was from God.

God had stepped into the life of Mary through the creative activity of the Holy Spirit (1:18). Then God took the initiative with Joseph through instruction and guidance (1:19–21, 24–25). And finally God redirected history through the fulfillment of prophecy (1:22–23). In Jesus, God had again manifested His presence in Israel by sending a Deliverer. All of our history is in God's hands, and Jesus is the final goal of history.

In the mysterious conception of Jesus in the virgin Mary, God took the initial step in our salvation to give us a Savior, a Redeemer, and a King. In some miraculous way the Holy Spirit brought together in the body of Mary the fully divine and the fully human, and the Incarnation took place.

The first step in our salvation.

Christians have always emphasized the costliness of Christmas to God the Father, Son, and Holy Spirit. God the eternal Son left the presence of the Father to take on human nature as Jesus of Nazareth. God was in Christ from the moment of conception onward to reconcile the world to Himself. God's sacrifice lasted for thirty-three years, and God's suffering didn't just begin on a Friday afternoon when Jesus died on the cross. Rather, God's suffering began at the conception and birth of Jesus, lasted throughout His ministry, and only ended after the resurrection of Jesus.

Artist Holman Hunt has depicted for us the shadow of the cross that hung over Jesus from His conception in Mary until His resurrection years later on Easter Sunday morning. Hunt's painting portrays a young Jesus in the carpenter's shop in Nazareth. In the picture, "The Shadow of Death," Jesus rises from a cramped position at His work bench and flexes His arms to work out the stiffness in them. As He stretches out His arms, He casts on the wall behind him the shadow of a cross. Hunt intended us to see that the Incarnation of Jesus was a sacrifice from beginning to end.

While Matthew focuses our attention on Mary, he does not linger there. He does want us, though, to identify with

This panel depicts the adoration of the Wise Men and is in the Church of the Nativity in Bethlehem. The town is situated about six miles south of Jerusalem. At the time of Jesus' birth it was on an important road to Hebron and the Negev.

the simple faith and trust of this sixteen-year-old peasant girl. She knew that if she obeyed the Lord and agreed to a pregnancy by the Holy Spirit she would bring trouble on herself. After all, Joseph might be so hurt that he would break their betrothal (which he nearly did), and she would have to rear a fatherless child amidst village scandal. Her trust in God gave her courage and she was willing to brave any pain to be the mother of the Messiah.

Jesus was born in Bethlehem, a small town on a gray limestone ridge five miles south of Jerusalem (2:1–8). I have visited Bethlehem a number of times and love to join my fellow pilgrims on Christmas Eve in Manger Square to celebrate the birthday of Jesus. I've never hesitated to travel one-third the way around the world to visit the cave-like stable where tradition says that Jesus entered history. Yet Herod the King would not go five miles to meet the newborn baby. But more than miles separated Herod from Bethlehem—too many murders stood between him and Jesus.

Any potential Messiah would have challenged Herod's rule. In 40 B.C. Herod had been made King of the Jews by the Romans. For over four decades of his rule he earned the title "Herod the Great" because of his forceful ability to keep order in a volatile country, the majestic buildings he constructed (including the temple in Jerusalem), and his unique managerial gifts. But he became equally renowned for his suspicious nature, and at the time of Jesus' birth, about six or seven B.C., he was known by the Jews as "a murderous old man." Herod killed many members of his own family—when his three oldest sons reached their maturity, he had them executed for fear they might rob him of his kingship.

Now, when crafty Herod heard about the Wise Men, he was deeply troubled. They had arrived in Jerusalem from the east after following a star for many miles which they believed was leading them to the birthplace of a new king. Herod hurriedly sent for them, heard their story for himself, and pretended to help them by asking the chief priests and the scribes where the Christ should be born.

Surely the religious scholars researched their sacred writings and were reminded by both Genesis 49:10 and Micah 5:2 that the Messiah would be born in Bethlehem— just a few miles down the road. They passed this word along to Herod, but beyond that these experts in the "Law and the Prophets" were apparently indifferent to the possible arrival of the Messiah. After all, they were probably certain that word wouldn't reach them through non-Jewish messengers.

But Herod wasn't the least bit indifferent. After all, a

The True King and the Wicked King (2:1–23)

The challenge to Herod's rule.

The arrival of the Wise Men.

17

new king would threaten his political position. And after reporting to the Wise Men what the Jewish scholars had said, he pretended that he was eager to worship the new king too. Herod then asked them to report back to him after they had found the babe.

Matthew continues the story and tells us the Wise Men found Jesus and Mary and Joseph living in a house. After worshiping the babe and leaving their gifts, they were warned by God in a dream not to go back through Jerusalem and report to Herod what they had found.

The flight to Egypt and Herod's act of murder.

It is possible that the Wise Men appeared on the scene almost two years after Jesus was born. So when Herod realized he had been tricked by them, he flew into a rage and ruthlessly ordered every baby two years and under in Bethlehem to be killed. But before this cruel edict could be carried out, God warned Joseph in a dream and gave him instructions to leave immediately for Egypt.

For centuries Jewish refugees had sought safety in Egypt from foreign armies invading Israel until there was a Jewish colony in every major city along the Nile River. So it seems quite logical that Joseph and Mary could find a temporary home there. For their brief stay in Egypt they would have had no trouble finding Jewish friends.

The return from Egypt.

After Herod's death Joseph was assured in a dream that it was safe to take his family back to Israel. Knowing that Archaelaus, Herod's son, was as vicious as his father and had started his reign by slaying thousands of influential people, Joseph, on the return trip, did not stop in Judea but hurried north to Galilee and settled down in Nazareth (2:19–23).

Galilee was looked upon by the religious orthodox in Jerusalem as "too gentile." The town of Nazareth was strategically situated near the Damascus-Egypt trade route and the highway from the Mediterranean seacoast to the east. Ideas, news, and goods moved through Galilee to and from the boundaries of the Roman empire. It was in this cosmopolitan atmosphere that Jesus grew up, exposed to a wide variety of cultures and philosophies. His horizons had to have been much broader than if he had been raised in Judea.

But here again we see that God's plan exceeded Joseph's imagination—and ours. For it was in this setting—in

A street scene in the old section of Nazareth near the area where Jesus spent His childhood. In Jesus' day Nazareth was a small village, and the houses were clustered together on the side of a hill—populated by craftsmen and farmers.

Nazareth of Galilee—that Jesus was exposed to a world view which later supported His message that the gospel of the Kingdom was for everyone, Jew and gentile alike; God's grace embraces the whole world.

As we look back over the first two chapters of Matthew we can see how he tried in several ways to express the uniqueness of Jesus. The genealogy shows Jesus as God's chosen One to fulfill the promises to Abraham and David. He would be a savior who surpassed the mighty Moses. For while Moses rescued the Jews from Egyptian slavery, it was Jesus who would deliver everyone who acknowledged Him as Lord from their sins. Moses gave his people the Law, while Jesus would eventually show us a Heavenly Father of love.

Texts from the Old Testament show Jesus to be the One promised to Israel by the prophets. And the homage of the Wise Men point to Him as King of the universe. His time in Bethlehem, Egypt, and Nazareth emphasize His significance for people from every nation. These are the dimensions in which Matthew wishes us to see Jesus. He was "God with us" from the beginning.

BOOK I

Matthew is now ready to begin the first of his five Books. Book I focuses on discipleship and introduces us to the initial steps of following Jesus—learning about and from Him and becoming like Him. For it is only after we become followers of Jesus that we become effective witnesses for Him.

Narrative ## *The Beginning of Jesus' Ministry 3:1–4:25*

In each of his five Books Matthew places a Narrative section and a Teaching section. In the Narrative he relates activities or events in Jesus' ministry. In the Teaching section Jesus teaches about the Kingdom of Heaven (or God) and draws out the deeper spiritual, practical, or theological meaning implicit in what He did in the Narrative section. Matthew's first Book includes chapters 3 through 7.

In Lesson One of our study we will look at chapters 3 and 4; in Lesson Two we will take up chapters 5 through 7, which comprise the Sermon on the Mount.

About 25–28 A.D. John the Baptist burst on the Jewish scene like a fire storm from the Old Testament announcing the new Kingdom and the dawning of the Messianic age (3:1–12).

The mood of the Old Testament had looked ahead to a time when the will of God in heaven would be done perfectly on earth. John had this picture in his mind when he preached that the Kingdom was near. Let us look now at the parts of this picture of the Kingdom as John saw them.

The Jews of John's day believed that the Old Testament prophet Elijah would return to be the forerunner and herald of the Kingdom. It was also believed that the dawning of the Kingdom would at first be a time of terror (Amos 5:18–20; Isa. 13:6–8; Joel 2:2; Zeph. 1:14–15). In the Jewish literature which emerged after 200 B.C. the writings about the Kingdom age became even more vivid in their descriptions of disaster.

Along with the picture of complete disintegration and harsh judgment as seen in the book of 2 Esdras 5:4–9 (in the Apocrypha), there was a positive vision about the Kingdom. During the dawning of the Kingdom all exiled Jews would be brought back to Israel, the ten tribes lost to Assyrian captivity in 722 B.C. would return, and Jerusalem would be restored and renewed. The land would be fertile once again, and war and strife would end.

When John preached about the Kingdom, these are the images that probably flooded the minds of his hearers. And as we get into our study of Matthew, we will see that Jesus built on this traditional Jewish picture of the Kingdom, but He also radically changed it into a new picture.

John called for a baptism of repentance—a turning away from sin—for Israel's religious leaders. Because of their venomous lives (3:7–9) they needed to flee from the coming judgment. He promised the Jews that if they did not repent, confess their sins, and be baptized with water, God would cut them off because of their unbelief. In every way, John's personality and message fitted the popular Jewish idea of a reincarnated Elijah who would be the forerunner of the Messiah.

But John's message said that there was much more

The Old Covenant Meets the New Covenant: John and Jesus (3:1–17)

involved than repentance. He said that when the Messiah came He would baptize them with fire and the Holy Spirit. Fire was the traditional symbol of pain and righteous wrath. The Messiah would be severe on them because of their sinful ways, but He would also give them the Holy Spirit, the very presence of God Himself to dwell in their lives. John also asserted that Israel had better get right with God and avoid the "wrath to come" (3:7).

The baptism of Jesus.   One day while John the Baptist was preaching down by the Jordan River, Jesus quietly moved out of the crowd and asked John to baptize Him (3:13–17). For thirty years Jesus had lived quietly in Nazareth, and now He was ready under God to begin His public ministry. And He did so by traveling south to the place near the Jordan River where John was preaching and baptizing.

The baptism of Jesus has always been difficult for us to understand. There were two elements in John's baptism—repentance of one's sins and an introduction into the new Kingdom that had just appeared in Israel's life. Jesus did not need to repent of any sin, so why did he need to be baptized? This is the question that evidently puzzled John.

I believe that Jesus insisted John baptize Him because He wanted to publicly identify Himself with the Kingdom John preached about. By contrast however, years later when the apostles baptized new converts into the church as Jesus had instructed them to do (28:19), Christian baptism had a far more profound meaning. For them and us baptism is based on the death, burial, and resurrection of Jesus and symbolizes that we have accepted the salvation that comes to us only through the Son of God.

Then, I believe John was puzzled for another reason. Jewish literature between the Old Testament and the New Testament had drawn a graphic picture of the Holy Spirit coming upon the Messiah in power like the roaring lion of the tribe of Judah. This was what John and his contemporaries expected. Instead, the Holy Spirit came upon Jesus like a dove, with gentleness—a radical departure from traditional expectations.

John was undoubtedly perplexed when he heard the voice of God announce from heaven, "This is my beloved Son, in whom I am well pleased." This quotation actually combines two short statements from two places in the Old Testament. Each phrase carries with it a complete and

The Jordan is the main river in Palestine. It originates in the Mount Hermon region, flowing south into the Sea of Galilee, and from there it flows 65 miles south to the Dead Sea. It was in the Jordan where Jesus was baptized by John.

totally different picture which had profound meaning for John the Baptist or any Jew who heard it.

"You are my beloved Son" is a quote from the second Psalm which clearly pictures Christ as a violently conquering hero as well as the coming King. This Psalm speaks of a militant Messiah who forces people to His way with a "rod of iron." This powerful, vengeful Messiah was what John and his contemporaries expected. For them this part of the quotation came as no surprise.

But the words "in whom I am well pleased" is a phrase from Isaiah 42. These words give an entirely different picture of the Messiah and would have called to the mind of any first century Jew three other passages from Isaiah—49:1–6, 50:4–9, and 52:13–53:12. These verses picture a servant who spread the good news of God's salvation and who suffered for the sins of others, though innocent Himself.

By coupling the words from Psalm 2 where the Messiah was pictured a conquering hero with the words from Isaiah where He was pictured a suffering servant, God had sent a message that was deeply puzzling to John the Baptist.

In traditional Jewish thought the Messiah could not suffer, and if He did suffer He could not possibly be the Messiah. For John and his contemporaries a combined Messiah-Suffering Servant would have been a contradiction in terms. And yet the voice of the Father was saying that His Son was to fulfill His role as Messiah through suffering.

The True Messiah Meets the Popular Messiahs (4:1–25)

Immediately after His Sonship was declared at His baptism, Jesus faced the challenge of his Messianic task—to call Jewish men and women into a new fellowship with God.

Jesus had confronted temptation at His baptism when John offered to change roles, "I have need to be baptized of thee." He rejected that ready-made leadership role because He knew it would turn Him into a pseudo-Messiah. Matthew now takes us from this temptation to the three classic temptations of 4:1–11.

The temptation of Jesus.

After His baptism Jesus entered the wilderness area between the Jordan River and Jerusalem. It was an empty and arid desert of jagged hills and warped landscapes. There, without human companionship or support, His faithfulness to the nature of His mission was tested. There, He faced the Satanic in its most personal form.

The tempter's first attack came after Jesus had been without food for forty days and was hungry. Satan suggested that He satisfy His hunger by turning the stones on the desert floor into bread. This was a challenge to Jesus to become a Messiah-Provider—to meet the material needs of people.

Jesus knew that a Messiah who provided bread or material goods would be popular but unable to fulfill His spiritual mission. To be well fed physically and to be spiritually mature are not the same thing.

The tempter's second attack on Jesus challenged Him to become a Messiah-Priest and meet the needs of people by performing miracles. Some Jews thought they needed wonder-working signs from heaven to assure them of God's presence and daily guidance. Another Jewish dream of the Golden Age was that the Messiah would perform spectacular stunts regularly to demonstrate His power and encourage the faithful.

The scribes and Pharisees had elevated this need for external confirmation—signs and wonders—into a doctrinal position. If Jesus could jump from the Royal Porch of Jerusalem's Temple and drop 450 feet to the Kidron Valley floor below without harm, as Satan suggested, He could by this stunt prove He was the Messiah and claim His national leadership. But Jesus knew that we could not live by exotic signs and wonders alone even if they came from God. Faith in wonders can become a substitute for faith in God. We can become slaves to the theatrical and even get to the point where we dictate to God what signs we will accept from Him.

There is an intriguing subtlety to this temptation in its application to our lives. Quite foolishly, I believe, we have in our church life allowed our heads to be turned by the bizarre and the sensational. Our trust is placed so often in the attraction of exotic buildings and catchy programs headlined by "superstars." We have developed a crowd mentality, believing that size spells success, and we burn ourselves out in a frantic effort to program the unusual.

But the subtlety here is the temptation to accomplish good with the wrong methods. It is also true that the Christian's God-given mission is to win people for Christ. But the model Jesus has given us to do this is not showy or gaudy.

It is true that in His effort to help people Jesus often did the miraculous, but He tried to avoid publicity. Our task is to be willing workers in the Kingdom of God right here in our world, not to be show people.

The tempter's third attack on Jesus challenged Him to become a Conqueror-Messiah and meet a yearning for political security. Here Satan took Jesus up to a high mountain and offered to give Him all the kingdoms of the world if He would bow down and worship him. Now, if the Conqueror-Messiah controlled all of the world's governments and political systems, then another Jewish dream would come true. Their longing for the restoration of a world patterned after the grand days of King David's military rule would be realized, and they could once again run rough-shod over the gentile nations.

Had Jesus given in to this temptation He would have played directly into the hands of the Zealots—a political party made up of cloak-and-dagger agents and terrorists who used violence against Rome's oppression of Israel. Force, guile, bribery, and power politics were all fair game to the Zealots.

But Jesus knew that while patriotism can make us a better people, nationalism usually makes us narrow and bigoted. Now, as then, the Kingdom of God cannot be compromised by power tactics and coercion. For to compromise with the world is to become *like* the world.

There in the Judean wilderness, Satan, with great skill, attempted to sabotage Jesus' mission, but He turned His back on the popular pseudo-Messiah ideas. First, Jesus rejected the role of an economic Messiah because it left other basic human needs untouched. Then He refused the miraculous route because it violated the character of God. And finally He turned down the invitation to pursue political power because it cannot redeem the whole person.

Jesus' temptation experience shows us how to resist and overcome the devil's attempts to defeat us. In each case Jesus responded to Satan's subtle suggestions by using Scripture, God's Word.

The beginning of Jesus' ministry.

Matthew next turns our attention away from the inner struggle in the wilderness to outer dangers and changes. After John the Baptist was arrested and imprisoned in Judea, Jesus traveled north to Galilee and established His headquarters at Capernaum on the north shore of the lake (4:12–17).

Capernaum was a city of about 15,000 people. There were eight other cities around the lake of about equal size, and approximately 300 commercial fishing boats worked the deep waters. All together the Galilee area covered about 1,250 square miles and contained 200 small cities.

Galilee was populous, prosperous, busy, unconventional, and open to a wide variety of new ideas because of its heterogeneous population and its strategic location on the main trade routes of the Middle East. We see here a hint of the future missionary movement to non-Jews as Jesus is at home in "Galilee of the Gentiles."

It was in Capernaum and the Galilee region that Jesus

declared the message of the imprisoned John the Baptist. He began to preach, "Repent, for the kingdom of heaven is at hand" (4:17). By "repent" John had meant that Jews should leave their sin and prepare for the coming Messiah. Jesus used the same message, but He gave it a wider application. For Jesus, the message called for Jew and gentile alike to identify with Him as the true Messiah and Savior.

Then too, Jesus' call to "repent" was an appeal for a new type of disciple (4:18–22). His strategy was to develop a disciplined community to live beside Him, identify with Him, change under Him, and learn from Him. In these verses we see Jesus selecting four of His followers—Peter, Andrew, James, and John—as He walks among the fishing boats anchored along the shore of the Sea of Galilee. It is possible that they had been disciples of John the Baptist and already knew something about Jesus. At any rate, Matthew wanted his original readers and us to see their immediate response to Jesus' magnetism and authority when he wrote, "they straightway left their nets, and followed him" (4:20).

Selecting the first disciples.

While we don't know what Jesus was looking for when He selected these disciples, they possessed certain traits which must have been attractive to Him. First, it is obvious that they were doers—they were men who got things done. Second, none of them were isolated recluses; they were at home in the busy world of men who ran the affairs of Galilee.

It is also apparent that they were accustomed to team work. Cooperation was a way of life—they knew how to lead and how to follow. And third, these men were hunters. They knew the exhiliration of fishing with giant nets from open boats at night, and they accepted the hazards of the work. These are not descriptions of flaccid men—they had to be activists and risk-takers to be successful.

I have to believe that the pattern hasn't changed over the last two thousand years. We can learn from these disciples' passion for action, their understanding of cooperation, their "hunter mentality," and their friendly openness to life and to other people. It is true, of course, that they were also intensely human. But because of their love for Jesus they kept trying and growing.

In the closing verses of this fourth chapter we see Jesus'

Jesus' strategy for ministry.

27

strategy for taking His good news to the people. He toured the scores of synagogues in Galilee, teaching, preaching, and healing the people He met there.

Jesus' missionary tour of Galilee established the pattern for all later missionary activity from the time of His disciples to the present. Centuries later, David Livingstone, the famous medical missionary to Africa, remarked that God had an only Son, and He too was a missionary and a physician.

Heavenly Father, Thank You for helping me understand this lesson. Please help me now to repent for Your Kingdom is yet at hand. Make Your Kingdom more real to me today, Lord, than my refrigerator, or my spouse. Let me repent, and then feel Your Presence.

WHAT THIS SCRIPTURE MEANS TO ME—Matthew 1–4

As I read this Scripture lesson, I was reminded of my mother-in-law's red felt bag. She regularly dropped into it the coins she received for change at the market.

Every two or three months my husband and I would pack up our three children and make the trip to her home. Sometime during our visit, out would come the red bag, clinking, fat and heavy with change. Each child was offered one reach into the bag with the promise that he or she could keep all the coins one tiny fist could hold.

As I dip into Matthew 1–4 I feel like the children must have felt. What riches! More than I can hold!

There is treasure there that belongs to each of us in deeply personal ways.

Our very first touch meets with gold. In the genealogy of Jesus we find His relatives are surprisingly like our own. Some are outstanding, some are ordinary, some are associated with sin and scandal, and some are a strong mixture of both good and bad.

Yet from them, through the power of the Holy Spirit, came the Christ. With that same power our Lord can fashion something beautiful out of our own broken humanity. John the Baptist expresses a similar idea with his words, "God is able from these stones to raise up children to Abraham."

For those who feel hopeless, either because of their own imperfections or those of their relatives, there is in the lineage of Jesus an incredibly beautiful, freeing message.

A book I loved as a child, titled *The Little Princess*, tells the story of an orphaned girl in London. At one point, carrying out an errand as a servant on a bitterly cold winter evening, she pauses before the lighted window of a bakery. Inside she sees a shelf heaped with warm buns. Shivering and half-starved she looks at them longingly. Then she happens to see a small coin which has fallen into the gutter. Suddenly one of the warm buns can be hers.

Through the lineage of Jesus we see how we need never stand in the cold, outside looking in. He is the coin. Through Him we are taken in and warmed. He is the Bread that restores us body and soul.

The name Emmanuel, "God with us," is part of the treasure found in these verses.

I saw a painting which poignantly illustrated how our Lord is with us in real-life situations. In the painting, a modern day businessman faces a desk piled high with paperwork. There is no Madison Avenue stylishness about his office; no carpet, no color coordination. A file cabinet, a desk, a chair, and his towering paperwork comprise the bleak setting. Clearly, he is there to do a considerable amount of hard work. But he is not alone. Behind the man, standing quietly, is Jesus.

Once more we touch gold in the wonderful story of the Wise Men. They were men who lifted their eyes to the heavens and sought the stars. When we look up to Him and seek the best, the highest, the finest, we find it. It was the Wise Men, not Herod, who were led to the manger.

We find yet more treasure in the account of Jesus' victory over temptation in the desert. He gives us a shining guideline to use in our own struggles with His rebuke to the devil: "You shall worship the Lord your God and Him only shall you serve."

A friend recently put it this way: "What it boils down to," she said, "is deciding who's 'Boss' in your life, God or self."

To choose as Jesus chose leads to blessings beyond measure.

LESSON 2
MATTHEW 5–7

The New Law

Jesus, Please open my mind to understand Your Word. Amen.

Teaching   Following the Narrative we have just studied, which describes the beginning of Jesus' ministry and shows us how to become disciples, is a Teaching section. Here we are shown in simple and colorful language how we are to act. This Teaching has been given many different labels, but it is most commonly known as the Sermon on the Mount. Matthew's Gospel is unique in many ways, but the Sermon on the Mount makes it distinctive.

In the Sermon on the Mount, three of the most popular chapters in the New Testament, Jesus gave His followers a pattern for behavior—a spiritual lifestyle that far surpassed the conventional pattern of Judaism and of even John the Baptist. At that time Jesus' words were revolutionary because they challenged the ordinary standards of Judaism by transcending outward behavior; they penetrated inner motives and attitudes. His listeners were challenged—no, commanded—to change their thinking about the Kingdom of God.

Matthew uses the expression "Kingdom" thirty-eight times. The Kingdom metaphor was clearly understood by Jesus' listeners though we are not especially familiar with it today. Because of their history and surrounding conditions they could identify with it.

They understood that God is King over the outer world

and the inner soul as well. The inner being (psychc) was as real to Jesus as the outer body is to us. To Jesus the Kingdom was within us, around us, among us, and in the future for us. It starts here and now and will be most fully realized in heaven. Its presence now reflects the greatness of Christ and its future fulfillment shows the Lordship of Christ.

We come now to a very familiar part of Matthew—the Beatitudes—"eight doors of joy." There didn't seem to be much joy in the religion of Jesus' day. The Sadducees and the Pharisees were obsessed with their religion of materialism and rigid rules. They were a rather somber lot. And the Zealots were also a joyless group as they exhibited their bitterness and hatred in acts of terror and revenge. It was a sorry scene.

But now Jesus wanted everyone to see that the gospel of the Kingdom of God is one of joy and blessedness. As His followers, joy and blessings are our birthright, even though there are those inevitable times of stress and difficulty.

Each Beatitude—each joy—portrays an attitude or action that will give us a taste of the Kingdom of Heaven here and now. As we move through these eight doors we will find a style of life that can give us a sense of happiness and inner joy which exceeds anything we could imagine.

So, in our imagination let's join Jesus and the disciples on the slopes of that mountain and listen to the eternal and life-changing truths the Master lays out for us.

Blessed are the poor in spirit—anyone aware of poverty of spirit and the need of wholeness (5:3). The Pharisees of Jesus' time concentrated so much on outer actions that they were blind to their inner, shadowy side. They were puffed up by their self-righteousness and achievement mentality and they were oblivious to the possibility of a deep and meaningful relationship with God.

On the other hand we know that we can't enter into God's presence on our own goodness; we can't manage our lives without God. We have discovered that life without God is a meaningless venture.

As "poor-in-spirit Christians," we can rejoice with a new, inner satisfaction given us by God in whom we have put our whole trust. We no longer turn to wealth, religious stunts, or political power to make our lives whole. On the contrary,

Eight Doors of Joy for the Disciple (5:1–16)

The Beatitudes.

The Sea of Galilee as framed through an arch in the Church of the Beatitudes, a traditional site of the Sermon on the Mount. The Mount is located a half a mile or so east of Capernaum and has a commanding view of the Sea of Galilee.

we have come to understand that as we place our complete reliance on God and trust Him fully, He can then act through us in working out His perfect plan for our lives.

Blessed are those who mourn—those who have deep feelings of sorrow over their own sins, care deeply about the shortcomings of others, and are remorseful over the knowledge that they have hurt God (5:4). Both John the Baptist and Jesus preached repentance to the religious leaders of Israel, but those leaders refused to acknowledge their sin in their relationship with God.

Jesus is telling us here that the Christian who has truly repented and is sorry for his or her sin is blessed by God. This is not to say that our thoughts, motives, and behavior will always be in tune with God's purposes for us and our world. But it does mean that as we live in daily awareness of the awful price Jesus paid for our salvation, we will always feel deep sorrow when we go against His will for us.

At the same time we are to always feel deep compassion for any and all who are suffering because of the consequences of sin in our world. We are to be a comfort-giving people. This was the Christian call and duty in the first century, and it is our call and privilege in these closing days of the twentieth century. Ours is a commitment to people, to their needs, to their hurts and fears.

I have a colleague who is a math teacher. Obviously, mathematics is neither Christian nor non-Christian. But, he says that he tries to be a Christian when he teaches. One time I asked him what he did when a student failed a test miserably and then came to his office with a sad story and asked him to reconsider and change the grade to a passing one. He said, "I commiserated with the student, but the 'F' still stood. Then I tried to be helpful and showed him how he could do better on the next test." My friend has experienced the comfort of God, and he in turn shares that comfort and compassion with others. That is what the good news of Jesus is all about.

Blessed are the meek—disciplined people whose lives are now God-controlled (5:5). In Jesus' day the rabbis had become overbearing in their learning, the Greeks were scornful in their intellectual pride, and the Romans were brutal with their military power. One way or another everyone seemed to be angry, and gentleness was a rare virtue.

Jesus tells us here that we are blessed if we are meek and our anger and passions are put under God's control. We acknowledge our poverty before God as we repent of our sin. We can be joyful because we have become gentle people who have received God's forgiveness. With His help we walk in grace and live in love. Like wild horses, we are bridled by the grace of God.

Moses is a superb example of how change can come by God's grace. Originally he had had a volcanic disposition, but he was tamed under the leadership of God (Numbers 12:3). He became a sensitive and kind man, having learned under God's guidance to handle the good as well as the bad. Even under the intensely trying conditions of leading thousands of unruly Israelites to the Promised Land, Moses consistently cared for their welfare and needs. The once arrogant aristocrat had become a meek and gentle man.

Blessed are those who hunger and thirst for righteousness— those who want to see God's right prevail with the same intensity of a starving person scrambling for food (5:6). Most of us who are studying this lesson have only a very superficial awareness of what it means to be ravenously hungry or tongue-swollen thirsty. But the people of tropical Palestine—Jesus' listeners—well understood the force of His words in this Beatitude, even as do millions today around the world who suffer the agony of daily hunger.

Jesus paints a vivid picture with a few words as He says we are blessed if our daily desire for righteousness and goodness is so intense that it is like a voracious hunger and a burning thirst. But unlike the Pharisees of Jesus' time we know that a hunger and thirst for righteousness cannot be satisfied by performing certain religious practices—by doing or not doing specific things. Rather, satisfaction and joy come from a passionate love for the Heavenly Father and a passionate desire to give of ourselves under the guidance of the Holy Spirit; to being people of righteousness at work against the inequities and suffering in the world.

Blessed are the merciful—those who feel the calamities of others are their own (5:7). Mercy, sympathetic understanding, and forgiveness are indeed central themes of the Gospels, and they stand in stark contrast to the religious mood of Jesus' time. But as people redeemed through Christ's death and resurrection, He has had mercy on us, and the word here is that we are to be merciful and compassionate to others. This is an essential quality of Christian grace.

The principle inherent in this Beatitude is of primary

importance to us in all our relationships. We are to be merciful and charitable with the attitudes and actions of everyone we come in contact with. The quality of mercy which Jesus commends here calls for us to be not judgmental or critical, for we don't usually know the circumstances of another person's life unless "we have walked a mile in his or her shoes."

Blessed are the pure in heart—those whose integrity is intact and whose motives are pure (5:8). In Jesus' day the religious leaders seldom acted with unmixed motives. The Sadducee always had one eye on your purse, so you clutched your money a little tighter when he was around. The Pharisee always had one eye on your sense of appreciation for his holiness, so you stayed alert to praise him for his piety. The Zealot always had one suspicious eye fixed on your political loyalties, so you were cautious about your patriotism when he was near.

As Christian disciples we are not to do anything out of guilt or obligation or as a means of bettering ourselves or to attract attention. Instead we are to strive each day to be motivated by our love for God and a selfless love for other people. We want the good and the true for no other reason than that it is the good and true.

Blessed are the peacemakers—those who bring people together in harmony and right relations (5:9). The Roman world of Jesus' time was supposed to be at peace. Caesar Augustus had imposed a military peace on the civilized world, the famous *pax Romana* or Roman peace. But while there was an absence of war, there was still an abundance of hostility.

An important teaching for us here, I believe, is that Jesus is not blessing those who merely prevent hostility, but those whose primary aim is to bring people together in right relationship. It is only as we have made our own peace with God and are at peace with ourselves that we are able to be at peace with others. And as our motives become pure with God's help, we are then able to better understand our neighbors in the next block and across the world because we know that God's love takes in everyone.

Blessed are those who are persecuted . . . for my sake—those who have deliberately shouldered the cross of Christ in the battle against the selfishness that determines so much of our behavior (5:10–12). Jesus was perfectly honest with the twelve disciples and with us. He warned that if we live by the first seven Beatitudes, we may well experience physical and emotional suffering.

None of us likes to be persecuted—to live in an atmosphere of suffocating suspicion, to have our privacy invaded by our critics, to be sniped at by those who disagree with us, to be misunderstood and penalized for alleged offenses. We want to be *liked*; God has created us to love and be loved.

When Jesus spoke out against the religious practices and standards of His day, He initiated a confrontation with the leaders of Judaism. Jesus modeled each of the Beatitudes to perfection, and yet He was hated and hounded to His death. Although he was "meek and lowly in heart" He was persecuted with unspeakable cruelty. And while most of us in the western world are not called upon today to endure physical persecution, if we follow the standard of goodness set here by Jesus, there will be those who attack us. In some instances those attacks will be motivated by guilt or envy or by self-righteous outrage over differences of opinion.

Why then, did Jesus say that we are to "rejoice, and be exceedingly glad" when we are confronted with pain and persecution of any kind? (5:12). That is a good question simply because the idea that we should be happy when we are confronted with opposition and persecution is radical—it jars our expectations. However, these words of Jesus are for us. So, let's look briefly at a couple of possible reasons.

First, when we are attacked because of our Christian witness it is probably because we are being effective. Dwight L. Moody, the great nineteenth-century American evangelist, said that when too much time went by without someone attacking him, he became concerned about the vitality of his message.

Second, as a rule, our greatest growth comes in times of opposition and persecution of one kind or another. When times are easy, our spiritual muscles atrophy.

We can rejoice because we share in a great fellowship and a great occasion. And while Jesus never promises that life will be easy, He does promise to be with us even in life's hard times.

Salt and light. Jesus follows His eight Beatitudes with two very colorful word pictures, "Ye are the salt of the earth. . . Ye are the light of the world"—those who have enriched, preserved, and influenced their world by being disciples of Jesus (5:13–16). In first-century Palestine, salt was perhaps the most common preservative. Jesus paid the twelve disciples and us a great compliment by comparing us with salt, which purifies, preserves, and flavors. As salt-disciples, our role is to give the world flavor and zest. This is no place for insipid Christians.

Jesus was not fire as John the Baptist wanted Him to be, but He was light. In John 8:12 He said, "I am the light of the world." Here He says *we* are the light of the world, but that is only possible as we reflect Him. As His disciples, we are guides, examples, models of goodness, and warning lights to the world. And as joyful disciples, we are to be winsome, charming, and attractive—but always drawing attention to Christ.

Five Doors to Spiritual Maturity (5:17–28)

At this point in the Sermon, Simon Peter may have interrupted Jesus to blurt out, "But as disciples how do we relate to the Law of Moses?"

Jesus then told the twelve that the Old Testament books were sacred, but He objected to the way the scribes and Pharisees were interpreting them with their legalistic traditions. Through the centuries there had grown up a whole collection of material, both written and oral, which gave interpretations to the Scriptures that Jesus refused to accept as from God. He further insisted that His teaching revealed the true meaning of the Law and the prophets. And Jesus then selected five issues from the Law to illustrate His point (5:17–20).

Cope with resentments.

The first example that Jesus used has to do with how to handle feelings of anger and hatred and how to achieve a new spirit of good will (5:21–26). He referred to the old commandment given at Mt. Sinai, "Thou shalt not kill," and then expanded it to include anger against a brother. Here Jesus got beyond overt acts of murder and pointed to the three inner steps that lead to violence: lingering over an injury (brooding); a refusal to be pacified (contempt); and plotting revenge (murder in the heart).

His point was that overt crimes are the results of inner deliberations. It is this inner anger and hidden hatred that must be exposed and eventually relinquished.

It is true, of course, that Jesus was speaking to a cancerous mood in first-century Palestine. But there is an equally important message here for us. As Christians, we cannot afford to harbor hostile, angry feelings toward anyone, and when misunderstandings do occur, we are to take the initiative in reconciliation.

This teaching also implies that we are not to attack other people in or out of the church for so-called holy motives. To Jesus, reconciliation was more important than even religious rites. People came first. Bernard M. Baruch was so right when he said that two things are bad for the heart—running up the stairs and running down people.

Covenant keeping vs. marriage breaking.

Jesus' second example of the new high standard for the twelve disciples and for us dealt with "marriage breaking" (the meaning of the word "adultery"). In our relationships with others we are not only to be free from anger, we are to be free from lust (5:27–32).

The sixth commandment given to Moses on Mt. Sinai read, "Thou shalt not commit adultery," but Jesus takes us beyond the act and warns against lustful looks and thoughts. We are to see each other as sons and daughters of God and not as bodies to be used for illicit satisfaction. For the Christian sexual responsibility is mandatory in attitude as well as in action.

Next, Jesus resorts to rather strong and colorful language when He says, "If thy right eye offend thee, pluck it out" and "If thy right hand offend thee, cut it off." The meaning for us here, I believe, is that we are to forcefully get rid of any thought or action that could lead us to sin.

Here also, because of the frivolous attitude toward the marriage relationship that had crept into Jewish practice, Jesus spoke out boldly against marriage breakup and divorce and flashed before us God's perfect pattern. We are neither to marry hastily nor take the marriage covenant lightly.

Honesty is the only policy.

The critical issue in Jesus' third example was truthful speech. Jewish teachers had always insisted that their people tell the truth, and especially if that truth was backed up by an oath. If someone made a promise using the name of God, it was taken seriously (5:33–37).

But in the time of Jesus many Jews were taking oaths when they really weren't necessary. In doing so they trivialized sacred language and tradition. Then there were those who deliberately omitted God's name from an oath because they had no intention of ever keeping their promise. They were purposely vague. But here Jesus makes the point that God cannot be eliminated from any promise, whether we use His name in it or not. He insists that we be honest in all of our dealings. Honesty, is the outward expression of an inner integrity.

Jesus presents before us here an idea that is very practical. As Christians, our character and inner motives are to be so shaped by God that backing up our word of promise by taking an oath becomes unnecessary. A high standard? Yes, but it is the Christian way.

Jesus is speaking now (5:38–42) to a response of the human heart that is as old as earliest history—the "eye for an eye and a tooth for a tooth" syndrome—get even for real or imagined hurts. We find it referred to in the early Jewish Scriptures (Lev. 24:20), and it also appeared in early Babylonian law over two thousand years before the time of Jesus.

Free to reject revenge.

But again, Jesus taught the need for a new attitude of non-resentment and non-retaliation. Jesus' example of "whosoever shall smite thee on the right cheek, turn to him the other also" has always held a fascination for both Christians and non-Christians. What was Jesus really telling us? I believe He was saying that as Christians, disciples of the Lord, our dignity is rooted in a personal relationship with God. Knowing that we are made in the image of God and enjoy a relationship with Him, we can be confident that we are of infinite worth to our Heavenly Father. With this assurance, nothing can demean our self-image. This frees us to "turn the other cheek" rather than allow the poison of bitterness and revenge to kill our spirits.

This section of our lesson closes with some of the most startling and provocative statements found in the Sermon on the Mount (5:43–48). Here Jesus says, "Love your enemies, bless them that curse you, do good to them that hate you, and pray for them which despitefully use you, and persecute you." As impossible as it may sound on the surface, this command of Jesus is at the very core of our relationships with other people.

Hate yields to invincible good will.

There are several Greek words for love, but the one used here is *agape*—not an emotion of the heart but an act of the

39

will—a state of mind whereby we wish for our "enemies" unreserved good will. This love is based on the nature of our Heavenly Father whose love is indiscriminate and all-inclusive. If we have confidence in God, we can renounce our own security and reach out in open friendship even to those who don't seem to like us.

When Jesus says that we are to pray for our enemies, He means that we are to see them as God does—with Fatherly good will. And as we with God's help are able to do that, our own feelings of ill-will and suspicion will be replaced by a God-given love that, hopefully, can restore a ruptured relationship. Spiritual health and wholeness become possible for us only as we catch the spirit of these words of Jesus.

Maria Goretti, an eleven-year-old girl who was fatally stabbed while resisting the advances of a nineteen-year-old youth, prayed these words as she lay dying, "May God forgive him! I want him in heaven." Maria's prayer captured the deep meaning Jesus wanted us to understand in these six verses.

The Right and Wrong Motives in Three Spiritual Practices (6:1–18)

In this section of the Sermon on the Mount Jesus teaches the twelve disciples and us how to improve our relationship with God. The Jews of Jesus' day practiced the presence of God by exercising three most important religious devotions: giving alms (money), praying, and fasting. Every young Jew was trained in these three practices until they became second nature to him, and he would never have thought of neglecting any of them.

However, some Jews had hypocritically used these rituals to gain public praise for themselves instead of concentrating on their relationship with God. Some had used these forms of worship to display their piety and gain the applause of their peers. Jesus speaks against this show-off attitude and challenges us to be unselfish in our motives when we worship God.

Giving. Giving money to the needy was one of the three religious devotions of Judaism (6:1–4). One's piety was measured by the amount of money one gave to the poor and how often the offerings were made. But most good practices can be profaned if they are done for the wrong reasons. Jesus' attention to almsgiving in these verses signifies the considerable abuse of the practice at that time.

Those who made a display of their "charity" came to like the attention so much they soon forgot that God was even involved in their giving. Among the devil's most subtle wiles is causing us to do good things in order to make ourselves feel good, to impress the people in our church or community, or to "get ahead" socially or in our work.

Jesus wants us to continue the Jewish habit of sharing money, but He wants us to do it with pure motives and inconspicuously—"in secret." Christ has saved us for service, not for sensations.

Prayer.

Jewish liturgy supplied the devout with stated prayers for all occasions. Again, unfortunately, hypocritical motives had crept into the practice. Some Jews prayed loud and long in the synagogues and on the crowded street corners to impress the people who heard them. They were actors who went where they could find an audience. Their goal was public acclaim, which they got, but God meant no more to them after they prayed than before.

Jesus told His disciples and us that when we pray with a right spirit, our reward, if we want to call it that, is a new relationship with our Heavenly Father (6:5–8). As we surrender ourselves to God in faith, He gives Himself to us.

The disciples' model prayer.

The Lord's Prayer (more appropriately called the Disciple's Prayer) is the heart of the Sermon on the Mount (6:9–13). Nothing can be said or written about it that comes close to doing it justice. As the most beautiful prayer ever prayed, it is an example of our relationship to our Creator, and shows us how we are to approach God. It is a prayer that *all* of us can pray. The simple words of this majestic prayer have challenged Christians from the time of Jesus until now.

Let us now take a brief look at the words of this model prayer. It opens with the familiar words, "Our Father which art in heaven, Hallowed be thy name." When Jesus taught His disciples and us to say "Our Father," He meant that God is personally concerned about us and that we are a community of believers who look to Christ as our common Lord and Savior.

"In heaven" means that our loving Father is also our transcendent Creator who brought us into existence and sustains us now and forever. It also means that He deserves our respect and worship, and His name is to be treated differently from any other.

In our society names don't necessarily convey meaning—they have become codes to label faces with. But in Jesus' day names were very important because they indicated the essential character of a person. (The name Jesus, for example, means "savior.") But Jesus is saying here that we are to revere the name of God and make it hallowed by the way we think, the way we use it, and by our daily conduct. We can blaspheme God's name when we scorn Him in our thoughts, irreverently toss His name about in our speech, or lead a cheap, immoral life.

"Thy Kingdom come, Thy will be done in earth, as it is in heaven." Here Jesus teaches us to pray for God's full purpose to be done now in us, and then done everywhere and in everyone. When we do God's will gladly and willingly, we admit that we believe God knows what is best for us and that He will do it.

As we pray for God's will to be done, our words take on a very practical meaning. God's will is not done when we gossip about a neighbor or ignore those in need who are hungry and living in poverty. God's will is not done if our word cannot be trusted or we become involved in questionable money or business transactions. And God's will is not done when we bicker among ourselves about church practices and interpretations. But God's will is done as we attempt, with His help, to shape our lives according to the principles established by Jesus, and as we reach out in love to others and share the good news of our salvation. It is then that God's Kingdom becomes a reality in our lives and in our worlds.

"Give us this day our daily bread." The request for bread focuses on our needs for today and tomorrow and tells us that God cares for our bodies. We understand that this is a petition for literal bread (and corn and sweet potatoes!) for our dinner table as well as the more general physical and spiritual needs that we have.

This prayer teaches us that we are not to ask for a lifetime of security. Rather, we are to live a day at a time and trust God for every need.

Also, this petition teaches us that we cannot pray selfishly. It is not just *my* bread, but *our* bread, that I am to pray for. As I receive bread, I am to share it with those who don't have any. We are all members of one family, and part of being a Christian is learning how to pass the bread from our Father to our brothers and sisters.

"And forgive us our debts, as we forgive our debtors." Our sin is an unpayable debt to God, but we avail ourselves of His forgiveness when we forgive those who have wronged us. I have always been sobered by the thought that *we are guilty of the good we don't do.* God gives each of us some capital (talents or gifts) to invest in life for our own spiritual growth and for the benefit of others. If we misuse our capital or deliberately squander it or unconsciously neglect it, our spiritual growth is stunted and we are unable to minister to others as God intended. We create a *debt* both for the things that we have done and the things we have left undone.

Asking for forgiveness presupposes that we forgive others. We cannot grow in our Christian walk and be spiritually renewed if we hold grudges and harbor resentments. Only as we forgive others are we able to receive forgiveness from others and from God. As we pray this prayer, we become conscious of where we have fallen short, and this in turn enables us to forgive those (parents, friends, etc.) who have failed us in any way.

"And lead us not into temptation, but deliver us from evil." This petition does not imply that God is trying to lead His people astray. God doesn't seduce anyone to evil (see James 1:13–15). Rather, this is a very positive statement asking God to give us the good instead of the evil. Jesus knew of the proud prayers of the self-righteous who were always inviting God to test them in order to prove their goodness. But He warns us against praying that kind of puffed-up prayer. Instead, we are to ask God to deliver us from the temptations that already surround us.

The implication from this part of the prayer is that we may ask the Father to give us wisdom before the testing time comes. And we may also ask Him to be with us during the test, and then to help us learn what we need to know once it is over. Temptations and times of testing are designed to make us stronger and better children of God. It is not a sin to be tested. Rather, we sin only when we fail the test.

"For thine is the Kingdom, and the power, and the glory,

forever. Amen." These final words of the Lord's Prayer are not a petition but an affirmation of God's power and authority. God's glory is also the primary motivation for everything we do in our Christian life and walk.

Fasting. We come now in our study to Judaism's third act of religious devotion (6:16–18). People fasted to focus their attention on God, to overcome distractions, to prepare their hearts for some word from God, and to repent of sins—both personal and national.

But again, there were those who latched on to fasting as a showy sign of superior piety. And to make sure that everyone knew they were fasting the hypocritical Pharisees would dust their faces with white ashes. While there are undoubtedly spiritual benefits from the discipline of fasting, it is quite likely that this pretense of righteousness did not—and does not—bring spiritual enrichment.

Quiet devotion and self-discipline enrich the inner life, not outward exhibition. Without intending to, we may fall into the Pharisees' trap of publicly displaying our holiness by parading what we do or don't do in order to gain acceptance and affirmation.

Growing in Faith (6:19–34)

Jesus now turned His attention in the Sermon on the Mount to the everyday worries and concerns of His disciples. Here He gives them and us practical advice on how to handle our worries and anxieties, and He encourages us to relax and put our complete trust in God's ability to supply our needs. First, He said, we need to choose the right goals or values in life (6:19–21). His advice here contrasts sharply with the choices made by the religious leaders of that time. The Sadducees had chosen money, the Pharisees wanted popular praise, and the Zealots struggled for political power. But none of the three was a proper goal or base for spiritual growth.

Our goals in life reflect our values. The things we want most demand all our energy and attention. This is why it is so important for us to subordinate all of our values to God's purposes and to choose His will as our central purpose in life.

Jesus also tells us here that to accumulate material things as ends in themselves is sheer folly. Things can always wear out, erode, or be stolen. And there is certainly nothing to be gained by being the richest person in the cemetery.

"Consider the lilies of the field, how they grow; they toil not, neither do they spin." In Jesus' day the people spun their own thread for clothing much as this modern Bedouin woman is doing.

While touring Southeast Asia, two wealthy Americans saw a boy pulling a crude wooden plow through the rice paddies while an old man guided it. When they inquired about the unusual sight they were told that the village church had been destroyed during the war. This poor but devoted Christian family had sold their ox to get some money to help rebuild their church. This was why they now pulled the plow themselves. When the Americans marveled at the sacrifice, they were promptly told that the farmers felt privileged that they had had an ox to sell. They understood the challenge of Jesus to invest our all for the building of His Kingdom.

In verses 22–24 Jesus points to the importance of integrity and singleness of purpose in our Christian walk. But to fully understand what Jesus means here we need to know that in New Testament Greek the reference to the eye being single refers to generosity—generosity with material goods and in our attitudes toward others. By contrast, an "evil eye" refers to a grudging and stingy attitude—one that is always lusting for the goods and good fortune of others.

In verse 24 when Jesus says "Ye cannot serve God and Mammon," He is referring to the Chaldean money-god, "Mammon." Jesus used this old pagan deity to give us another warning—the one sure escape from the tyranny of "things" is to submit our values and lives to the rule of God. He is not underestimating the importance of money in our lives, but He wants us to see that it must not have first place.

And John Henry Jowett, that great preacher of the past, had things in proper perspective when he said, "The real measure of our wealth is how much we'd be worth, if we lost all our money."

In verses 25–34 we find some powerful, encouraging words for us living in these complex days of the late twentieth century. He is talking about anxiety and worry—surely a problem in first-century Palestine but a crippling disease of our time.

But here in colorful language we read that even as God has provided for birds and flowers and all of nature, He has provided amply for our welfare as well if we will trust Him, "And why take ye thought for raiment? Consider the lilies of the field, how they grow; they toil not, neither do they spin" (6:28). We are assured that our loving Heavenly

Father knows our needs and will supply them as we seek first His Kingdom and righteousness. True, we are to do what we can, but then we are to leave the future with Him.

But most of us find these words of Jesus hard to accept and follow. Our faith and trust in God is weak when it comes to providing for our temporal needs even though He has faithfully demonstrated His care for us through the years. Because of our lack of trust we spend time spinning our wheels unnecessarily. But here Jesus has said, "Take no [anxious] thought for your life—don't worry, trust God."

The Disciple and His Decisions (7:1–29)

In these closing verses of the Sermon on the Mount Jesus gives His disciples and us some wise advice about making decisions consistent with our discipleship. Our choice to follow Jesus is the most crucial decision that we could ever make. But giving our life to Him is only the first of many decisions that we must make in our Christian pilgrimage.

In this section Jesus directs our thinking to six different areas which require attention in our quest for spiritual maturity. Jesus gives us good advice in these verses, but He leaves the final decisions to us. We are free to remain infant Christians and we are free to grow in faith. However, the consequences of failing to mature are also one of Jesus' themes in this seventh chapter of Matthew. But now, let's turn our attention to the first words of advice in this chapter; they concern our attitude toward other people.

Judge not.

In emphatic language Jesus says, "Judge not, that ye be not judged." Don't be judgmental (7:1–6)! These were sharp words to His listeners, and everyone recognized the prime targets, the Jewish religious leaders, who had a "We judge; you behave!" attitude.

There's an urgency in these words because legalism is harsh and judgmental. It is a deceptive, and crippling malady that inhibits spiritual development and growth. The Pharisees of Jesus' day were extreme legalists imprisoned by the narrowness of their own rules and interpretations. But unfortunately, there have always been Pharisee types, and they exist today. All of us, though, will do well to guard against any hint of this attitude in our own lives.

We are all called upon to make judgments and ethical appraisals. But what Jesus is forbidding is sharp-tongued, acid criticism, censoriousness, and scapegoating. We fail

47

as judges when we use one standard to measure ourselves and a much higher standard to judge our neighbor. In verse three Jesus calls on His own carpenter background, and with a marvelous touch of humor He says that we appear silly as we strain to pick a speck of sawdust or a splinter out of someone else's eye when we have a two-by-four in our own eye.

The message here for us is that God has not appointed us as judges over others. We're not qualified to assess the motives and actions of our neighbor, fellow church member, employer, or employee. The consequence of being judgmental does not hurt others, though. It damages us, for it produces an arrogant and pompous attitude which makes us unpleasant to be around.

Our calling as Christians is most certainly not to criticize others but to share with them our own experience and progress in the Christian life. But in the sixth verse Jesus' comment about not giving that which is holy to dogs and not casting pearls before swine admonishes us about how and when we share. His words were a graphic metaphor to His listeners which they surely recognized immediately.

For us, Jesus' admonition means that we are to use good judgment and discrimination about how and when to share our faith. If we approach less mature believers or non-Christians in the wrong way, it may affect them adversely. Thoughtless sharing and witnessing may actually do people harm and drive them away. We are to care enough about others not to force ourselves on them. And there may be times when it is far better to remain quiet. This was well illustrated when Jesus was questioned by Pilate. At a certain point He remained silent because He knew there was nothing to discuss with a governor who was determined to execute Him in order to protect his own interests.

Our fellowship with God.　　The graphic words in these verses give us a vivid picture of how we are to pray (7:7–12). Jesus' listeners knew a lot about prayer, but He wanted them to come to a new understanding—that the Heavenly Father was a God who loved them and who was not reluctant to answer. He longed to have fellowship with them and was eager to provide for their needs.

Few words have so electrified Christians over the centuries: "Ask, and it shall be given you; seek, and ye shall find; knock, and it shall be opened unto you." The initiative is ours; then God can respond without violating our freedom. Prayer is a cooperative activity.

But the catch is that we sometimes request the wrong things, and then we pout like little children when we don't get what we've asked for. Jesus tells us here that God is eager to respond to our needs even as a father wants to give his child the things that are good for him.

It is only as we grow and mature as Christians that we begin to understand what we need and ask accordingly. We are the ones who need to change, not God.

So often I've said, "Lord, thank you for not giving me what I begged you for two years ago. If you had, I'd be in a terrible mess today." We are most fortunate sometimes when God does not answer our prayers with a yes. But the important word here is that we are to pray because, as Dr. Alexis Carrel put it, "Prayer is the most powerful form of energy that one can generate."

Jesus now closes this paragraph on prayer with words that have since become known as the Golden Rule: "Therefore all things whatsoever ye would that men should do to you, do ye even so to them. . ." Though this command has often been misquoted and profaned, it is Jesus' standard for relationships. We begin to understand what this means when we see God doing good things for us. "Not as the law allows, but as love demands" becomes our motto.

Jesus counsels us about the kind of discipline we need in order to fulfill our commitment to Him as growing, maturing Christians in these two verses (7:13–14). He refers to the narrow way that will lead us to maturity and the broad way which will lead us to mediocrity. In our humanness we long for life to be easy and comfortable, but in our better moments we know that growth of any kind comes out of difficulty.

Life with discipline or without.

On the other hand the broad way symbolizes a life without any restraints, disciplines, or loyalties. But such a life fails to produce the joy and satisfaction that comes through healthy and creative achievement. The way of the athlete training for the Olympics is not broad and easy; it calls for single-minded discipline.

The entrance door to the Church of the Nativity in Bethlehem is very narrow, allowing only one person at a time to bend over and go in. It is difficult to enter and symbolizes the rebirth that avoids the broad and easy way.

This narrow door inside the Church of the Nativity is not the one referred to in the text. However, it does suggest the beauty of this ancient church—the oldest in Christendom. The star marks the traditional spot of Jesus' birth.

Jesus knows that we are not saved by our goodness, but He does not release us from the demanding work that we must do to grow up as believers.

Selecting spiritual leaders with care.

In this section (7:15–20) Jesus tells us how to practice religious discernment—how to differentiate the true and false. When He referred to false prophets, His listeners understood exactly what He meant. Israel's history abounded with counterfeit prophets. The first-century church was plagued with phony leaders. Gentile converts wanted to practice a freedom that would allow them to continue living morally lax. On the other hand, Jewish Christians were still trapped in their old legalism with suffocating rules about "do this" and "don't do that or God will be angry with you."

Our church today is caught in the same kind of conflicting teaching. We have our "false prophets" who teach an easy religion, and we have those who concentrate on a rigid legalism based on a system of "do's" and "don'ts." There may be qualities in both of these aberrations that have a gospel sound, but they are not the gospel as Jesus taught it.

Jesus very carefully points out that "by their fruits ye shall know them." It is their actions, not their words, that enable us to determine the integrity of our spiritual leaders and our brothers and sisters in Christ. We are not to be judges of others, but neither are we to be led astray by any form of false teaching. As we pray for God-given spiritual discernment, the Spirit of God will enable us to separate the true from the false.

The disciple's obedience.

In these verses (7:21–23) Jesus tells us that it is performance and not just our promise that counts in life. Demonstrating our faith, not just talking about it, is the challenge that Jesus lays before us here.

The Sermon on the Mount is not only for us to admire, but it is to become the guideline of our life. It isn't the repeating of creeds or the use of religious language that counts. Jesus made it plain that "not everyone that saith unto me, Lord, Lord shall enter the kingdom of heaven." But the true test of authentic discipleship is in "he that doeth the will of my Father which is in heaven." We may profess love, but if we don't act out love, our profession is false.

The disciple's solid foundation.

Jesus the master carpenter is also Jesus the master speaker, and He knows how to conclude a message by calling us to action (7:24–29). But even in doing that He leaves the final decision to us. We have heard His words—"these sayings of mine"—now we are confronted by a decision: will we *practice* "these sayings"?

Out of His intimate knowledge of carpentry and building houses Jesus speaks of the necessity of a rock-like foundation in our Christian life. His metaphor is a good one: our character is like a house. If we are thoughtful and wise, we will build our lives on a solid spiritual foundation. This then will give us a strong base from which we can handle anything that comes our way, even in these complex closing days of the twentieth century. With this kind of foundation life's hard times will not shake us.

A proper foundation and quality structure are crucial in construction and in life, Jesus tells us. If we are wise, we will build on His sayings and be obedient to His Word.

On the other hand we have the option of attempting to build our lives on a shifting, sandy, and unstable foundation. We can take the careless, easy way and cut corners, but in the story Jesus tells us here we are warned of the disaster that will result. The easy way ends in hard tragedy.

In the last two verses of the seventh chapter Matthew adds a postscript to Jesus' sermon—he gives us the reaction of the crowd. It must have been electric for he says that the people were "astonished" at Jesus' doctrine because He "taught them as one having authority."

Dear Jesus, I appreciate the guidance You've given me throughout this lesson. Your new law as expressed in the Sermon on the Mount certainly challenges me. Help me to walk the second mile; to love my enemies; to shine my light of love.

WHAT THIS SCRIPTURE MEANS TO ME—Matthew 5–7

When I read Matthew 5–7, the main threads glow like gold fibers woven through a tapestry.

Our Lord tells us we have a Father in heaven who loves us. He uses the word "father" seventeen times, as if by repetition to make us understand the intimate, loving relationship God longs to have with us.

He reveals our Father as one who cares about our very real personal needs. Thinking of how our Father cares for us, I remember a "lilies of the field" experience I had when I was a young mother.

The country was in an economic recession. Things were tight for us financially as well. Our children attended a parochial school because we valued the Christian environment it offered. However, because of our financial constraints, it became apparent that tuition payments for another year would be out of the question. The children were sorely disappointed.

"Isn't there some way?" one of them kept asking. The only way I knew was to go to our Lord. Together we prayed that, if there was a way, the Father would show us.

A few days later, when I went to pick up the children at school, one of the teachers came over to the car.

"I don't know what your reason is for not re-enrolling the children," she said. "But if it's financial, I've talked with the headmaster, and we'd like to offer them scholarships."

As I heard her words, a flash of joy surged through me, and I felt such an intense awareness of the Father's care. It had never occurred to me that the school had scholarship funds, but God knew. He had indeed shown us the way.

Jesus tells us of our Father's knowing what we need before we ask. Someone once called this aspect of God's love, "The love of God which goes before us."

For several years I have had a full schedule of commitments on my calendar. But one spring, looking ahead into the fall, I noticed my calendar was empty from September through November. This was most unusual, as the fall season was always my busiest time of the year. However, since I had earnestly prayed that our Lord would take charge of my commitments, I felt that somehow this vacuum must be of Him.

In the middle of the summer our oldest daughter came to us with the joyful news of her engagement. They had chosen a November wedding date.

"Clear your calendar from September through November," advised a friend. "You'll need every minute to prepare for the wedding."

She was right, but I experienced through those happy, busy days such a sense of "The love of God which goes before us." He had, in His wisdom, cleared my calendar for me.

Our Lord tells us that our relationship with the Father is to be close, so close that even our inmost heart is to be open to His guidance. He gives us guidelines on the way to live, not just in actions but in attitude and outlook.

Yet, as we seek to follow His teachings, we are often reminded of Brother Lawrence's prayer, "Lord, I cannot do this unless Thou enablest me."

Kay, a popular high school senior, discovered that another student was spreading false rumors about her. Her first reaction was anger and the desire to strike back. But she asked the Lord to help her forgive, prayed for the girl who had maligned her, and went out of her way to treat her graciously.

The Lord answered Kay's prayer by freeing her from feelings of bitterness, and she was inwardly at peace. Then, to her surprise, the girl stopped spreading the false rumors and became, if not a friend, no longer a source of hostility.

We are not alone, nor adrift. We have a Father who loves us, walks with us, and shows us the way. Our striving spirits can come home to rest in Him.

LESSON 3
MATTHEW 8–10

Concerning Apostleship

BOOK II

Heavenly Father, Please help me to learn about You. AMEN.

In our last lesson, Matthew showed us in the Narrative and Teaching sections how to become and act like disciples. As disciples of Jesus we are His students and followers. In this lesson, Matthew leads us into the deeper experience of becoming an apostle, a living witness for Jesus.

In a Narrative collection of miracle stories (Chapters 8–9) Matthew shows us how Jesus conducted His healing ministry. He demonstrated God's power by curing the diseased, casting out demons, raising the dead, and calming destructive forces of nature.

In Chapter 10, Matthew shows us in the Teaching section how Jesus turned the twelve disciples into apostles, authorized their missionary activities, and gave them their instructions. Jesus appointed them the tasks of carrying out the compassionate ministry of preaching, teaching, and healing that He had so ably modeled before them.

At the same time, we discover by the example of Jesus and the twelve disciples what He can do for us in our own Christian pilgrimage. We can see that it is His plan for us to make the giant step from being his students—disciples—to being his missionaries—apostles—to our twentieth-century world.

Jesus' Mighty Works, 8–9

In the ten miracle stories found in the eighth and ninth chapters of Matthew the authority of Jesus is a major theme. In the Sermon on the Mount Jesus *taught* us with authority. Now, in these miracles He *acts* with authority.

With artistic and theological design Matthew divides the ten miracles in Chapters 8–9 into three groups with three miracles in each group. A fourth miracle is inserted into the narrative of the last three.

Healing the Three Unacceptables (8:1–22)

In the first miracle Jesus cured an "untouchable" leper (8:1–4). In the time of Jesus a leper was regarded as hygienically and ritually unclean. He contaminated anything and anybody he touched. Next to a corpse, a leper was thought to be the most defiling thing an orthodox rabbi could touch. By the Law (Lev. 13:45) a leper was forced to shout "Unclean! Unclean!" when someone accidentally got near him. In fact, it was forbidden for anyone to get within six feet of a leper. And at all times the diseased outcast was required to wear torn clothing, let his hair hang loose, and cover his upper lip—these were all signs to warn off the unwary.

The healing of a leper.

But in this story, Jesus did the unthinkable and touched the untouchable. He felt secure in the knowledge that in the eyes of God there were no untouchables. And He was at ease with those whom the Law and tradition considered outcasts. We see in this incident that Jesus had no fear of disease and didn't hesitate to bend the Law to relieve human pain.

Incidentally, when you read the second verse, did you notice what the leper said when he approached Jesus? "Lord, if thou wilt, thou canst make me clean." In modern English he was saying, "Lord, if You want to, You can heal me." That is faith! Obviously he knew about Jesus, so he came believing. Immediately Jesus responded, "I will; be thou clean"—"Of course, I want to heal you"; and He did. This is just another instance among so many of Jesus' responses to human need.

Then Jesus asked the leper to do two things. First, he was to present himself to the priest as the Law required and get the certificate of readmission to society. By insisting that the ex-leper do this Jesus proved that He didn't come to abolish the Law and the Old Testament but to fulfill it and to teach others to keep its spirit. Second, Jesus asked the man to keep quiet about the source of his cure. He asked this because He wanted to avoid publicity. Jesus did not want the crowds to follow Him simply because of His miracles.

It is important for us to understand that in first-century Palestine rabbis were expected to heal the sick because they acted as local medical doctors. A rabbi's ability to heal was a sign of his spiritual power. But the people also believed that healing power could come from Satan as readily as from God. Evil arts ("black magic") could be practiced by a renegade rabbi, but a sure test of a rabbi's source of power was his loyalty to the Law.

For this reason the Pharisees never questioned the fact of Jesus' miracles; they only speculated the source of His power and His right to it (Matt. 9:34; 12:24). Therefore when Jesus asserted His authority over the Law by touching the leper, the Pharisees believed that Satan was His source of power. And a Satan-inspired rabbi deserved to be executed.

Jesus, of course, knew this, but once again He acted boldly to relieve human suffering in spite of physical danger to Himself. Here again, He gives us a model for our actions as Christians. There are people around us every day—in our neighborhoods, in stores, in offices—who are in desperate need of our compassion and love. In the crush and hurry of our urban and suburban worlds we merely brush against people who are lonely and hurting, who are wrestling with problems that threaten their emotional and spiritual equilibrium. They long for someone who will listen to them and act as if they care.

It is to these people, irrespective of their need, that we are called to span the "six foot" distance as Jesus did with this leper. We can bridge any chasm if we have the love of Christ in our hearts. It is to the hungry in New York's Bowery and in India's Calcutta that we are called to help. It is to the sick, the disease-ridden, the orphaned by little or big wars, and the displaced that we are to show the caring love of God. All of this is our Christian mission as we remember the words, "In as much as ye have done it unto the least of these, ye have done it unto me."

The second miracle story in Matthew's Gospel has Jesus rubbing shoulders with another untouchable—a gentile. For Jesus this association involved as much risk as touching the leper. The story of the unacceptable gentile (8:5–13) highlights for us the priority of compassionate service over nationalism. It also illustrates how Jesus reinterpreted the Law to show that God's love is for everyone.

Jesus heals the centurion's servant.

The centurion in this story was a Roman officer in command of one hundred soldiers. He was stationed at the garrison of Capernaum to keep the restless Galileans under control. When this Roman officer came to Jesus in behalf of his palsy-ridden servant, Jesus offered to go to his "unclean" house and heal the servant. But in an extraordinary flash of faith this disciplined military man insisted that his home was unworthy to have Jesus as a visitor. He said, "Speak the word . . . and my servant shall be healed." The centurion was a man of authority, he therefore recognized the authority that Jesus possessed.

Note Jesus' reaction, "I have not found so great faith, no, not in Israel." And then came the words from Jesus that electrified the centurion and that have changed lives ever since," . . . *as thou hast believed* so be it done unto thee" (italics mine).

What can we learn from this story that will help us as we go about our task of witnessing for Christ? First, we can see that there are lots of people outside the church who are ready and eager to believe in the power of Jesus. Like the centurion, they are just waiting for a word from us to push them in His direction. We can be the door that will open up new life for them.

Second, we can learn to respond to need as quickly as Jesus did. Jesus was ready instantly to go heal the servant. For Him a need was a command to be acted on at once.

Third, we see in this story that Jesus was delighted over the centurion's faith—He marveled and was joyful. Our witnessing for Christ has a kind of built-in gladness that makes us delight in the faith of others when they come to Christ.

Fourth, we learn the importance of faith. The centurion was supremely confident that Jesus could heal his servant even at a distance, and his faith was rewarded when the servant was actually healed.

It is believed the home of Peter in Capernaum is possibly located beneath the octagonal building which appears in this scene—located near the Capernaum synagogue. Franciscan excavators substantiate this possibility.

And last, we learn that Jesus ignored the superficial lines between a clean Jew and an "unclean" gentile. Any person who has genuine faith is a soul-compatriot of the Old Testament patriarchs and the New Testament disciples. We see that background and nationality mean nothing when it comes to putting our trust in Jesus.

Jesus heals Peter's mother-in-law.

The third miracle in Matthew's Gospel might not seem extraordinary to us, but to the people of Jesus' day, what He did was unthinkable. Immediately following the episode with the Roman centurion, Jesus and His disciples went to Peter's home and discovered that Peter's mother-in-law was sick with a fever (8:14–18). Her illness might not sound particularly serious, but the area around Capernaum was a breeding place for malaria-carrying mosquitos, and it is not unlikely that she had been infected by some of them. In an act of compassion for her misery Jesus touched her and she was healed.

Why was this so unusual? In Jewish society women were second-class citizens with few legal rights. Jesus' miraculous healing of Peter's mother-in-law signified the full equality of women with men. He saw her need and cured her with His touch.

What do we carry away from this scene to help us in our Christian walk? We see that Jesus thinks both men and women are equally worthy in the eyes of God. Here we learn that there are no second-class citizens in God's Kingdom.

Matthew then tells us that on the evening of that same day—the Sabbath, according to the Gospel of Mark—Jesus was besieged by the crowds. Again, in compassion, He healed everyone who had any kind of physical or emotional need in fulfillment of the prophecy in Isaiah 53:4, "...he hath borne our griefs, and carried our sorrows."

At this point in the Gospel, Matthew seems to interrupt the sequence with a brief interlude. Ever since the Sermon on the Mount and the miracle healings which followed, Jesus had acquired a mob of enthusiastic followers from all strata of Jewish life. They were attracted to Him because of His words and healings. But Jesus pauses now to tell a story to illustrate that His Way is costly and full of risk. The Christian way is not paved with cheap grace. A Harlem minister has often declared, "Salvation is free, but not cheap."

The story of the two reluctant men.

The first man, a scribe, swears his allegiance without qualification (8:18–20). Now, scribes represented the upper layer of society with its sophistication and security. So Jesus warned him, as He also warns us, that the Christian life is not made up of financial security and social acceptance. Instead, there is a cost to our discipleship.

The second man was a disciple but his hesitation to break with tradition betrayed his lack of commitment (8:21–22). This disciple who wanted to "bury his father" was a recruit from the countryside and accustomed to financial insecurity. Jesus laid down a completely different requirement to him. At first Jesus' response to his request might seem unreasonable since to look after aged parents until their death was one of the most sacred responsibilities among Jews under the Law. But for this man to delay following Christ until his father died could mean several years of lost opportunity. And Jesus' mission was immediate.

It seems to me that the story of these two reluctant men illustrates the need to thoughtfully and prayerfully establish our spiritual priorities. Most of us live out our lives working at our chosen job or profession, maintaining a home, raising our families, and functioning as responsible citizens in our little worlds. Our daily contribution to the stream of life is important. But there is also the danger that we may become so involved in both the routines and adventures of day-to-day living that our spiritual priorities suffer or are lost entirely. It is easy to get so distracted with life's legitimate concerns that we neglect our true mission as citizens of God's Kingdom.

The lesson for all of us in these two stories is simply this: whether we witness in the marketplace, at home, or in some foreign country, our priorities are to be fixed on Jesus Christ. And as for any other needs, we have the assurance of Jesus' words in the Sermon on the Mount, "...seek ye first the Kingdom of God, and his righteousness; and all these things shall be added unto you" (6:33).

Power Over the Dark Powers (8:23–9:17)

In this part of our lesson we turn our attention to the second group of miracles Jesus performed. Here He exhibited His authority over the power of nature, over demons and the underworld, and over the power of sin. Again, we find in His faith and actions a model for our lives and service.

Jesus calms the storm.

A violent storm swept down on Jesus and His disciples as they crossed the Sea of Galilee (8:23–27). The boat was sinking, the disciples were hysterical, and Jesus was asleep. In their panic they awoke Jesus and screamed out their terror to Him over the pounding of the wind and waves. First Jesus chided the disciples for letting their fear swamp their faith. Then He rebuked the storm "and there was a great calm." The water became placid. Jesus took control and asserted His authority over the elements of nature.

Matthew tells us that the disciples "marveled" over Jesus' power and exclaimed that "even the winds and the sea obey him." From our vantage point we marvel too, for without straining our imaginations we can see in this awe-

A storm threatens the Sea of Galilee as angry clouds form over the water. Because of the topography of the region such storms occur frequently now, even as when Jesus rebuked and calmed the sea when He and His disciples were in the boat.

some story a parallel in our own lives. Family problems, money concerns, job reversals, the ravages of disease, emotional breakdowns, betrayal by those we trusted, misunderstandings—all are storms that menace our lives and threaten our sanity.

I'm sure that when the storm struck the disciple's boat on the Sea of Galilee those seasoned fishermen in the group used every trick they knew to keep things under control, but when nothing worked, they panicked.

As it was with them, so it is with us when life's storms strike. So often we try to work things out with our own knowledge and power and out of our own resources. For example, I recall so well my feelings several years ago when I was crossing the Sea of Galilee from Tiberius to Capernaum in a small boat. Suddenly a storm began to brew and the waves got very choppy. Then as the velocity of the storm increased, I got more and more uneasy and fearful. In my desperation under the pressure of the moment I thought to myself, "I wonder what would happen if I stood up in the boat, raised my hand, and shouted, 'Peace! Be still!'" But just as quickly I realized how silly that would be—I could end up overboard. This was no time for poor judgment or foolish ideas. I realized again that, as always, I couldn't make it on my own.

As Christians, we don't make it on our own today any more than the disciples did on that frightening occasion. But so often in times of stress we too become fearful; it can be said of us, "O ye of little faith." The lesson for us here, though, is that even as Jesus calmed the storm on the Sea of Galilee with a word, He will calm the storms in our lives if our faith and confidence is in Him. And as we experience this miracle in our own lives, we in turn can become "storm calmers" for others whose lives are being battered and shattered by life's hard times.

Jesus heals two demented men.

Matthew now moves us across the calm sea to the eastern shore. The battle against the rampaging forces of nature has been won. But now, as they step ashore in the gentile "country of the Gergesenes," they are immediately confronted by a powerful and sinister force (8:28–34), "...there met him two possessed with devils, coming out of the tombs, exceeding fierce, so that no man might pass that way."

Once again we see Jesus in action. When He spoke with authority on the stormy sea, it became calm. Now as He looks with compassion on these two demented men, Jesus speaks a word and they are healed. In this scene Matthew shows us a Christ who is both authoritative and fearless in the presence of demons. Jesus orders the demons out of the tormented men into a nearby herd of swine.

For us, this may be the most difficult of the ten miracles to understand. But it is clear that Jesus felt the deliverance of those two demoniacs was more important than a herd of pigs. Jesus saved those men from the shackles of evil, and He wanted the people in the nearby town to share in the same experience. But unlike the two men, the townspeople refused to listen and not only turned their backs on Jesus but asked Him to leave.

I believe, though, that this unusual and perhaps difficult to understand miracle account has a very practical word for us. First, "the country of the Gergesenes" was in gentile country, east of the Jordan River and the Sea of Galilee. In this we see once again the universal compassion of Jesus. Healing was for everyone. The love of Christ is inclusive, not exclusive.

Second, I believe we see in this story a parallel between the violent insanity of these two men who were possessed with devils and the insanity that grips our world today. Our television news is full of violence and terrorism. It spews out stories of child abuse and wife abuse. The threat of the insanities of war bombard our senses. Our "we" and "they" mentality has us engulfed in suspicion and name-calling.

But the good news for us is that the same Jesus who healed those two insane maniacs has the authority and power to heal the insanities in our world today. As His disciples and apostles, we are called to be living witnesses to His redemptive power. Through our faith and actions we can make a difference in our own worlds. "I can do all things through Christ which strengtheneth me" (Phil. 4:13).

Matthew now moves us back across the Sea of Galilee to Capernaum where Jesus is confronted by a man who is tragically disabled by palsy (9:1–8). As the story unfolds, we discover that this man was sick outwardly because he was sick inwardly. When Jesus saw him, He knew the palsy was caused by a sin-dominated heart and life, for His first words were, "Son, be of good cheer; thy sins be forgiven thee." Jesus knew that until his mind and thoughts were cleared of the sin, his legs wouldn't carry him. Then in response to the heckling of the scribes, Jesus confirmed the inner spiritual miracle by saying, "Arise, take up thy bed, and go unto thine house."

Matthew tells us that the crowds who saw the miracle marveled and praised God, but the scribes accused Jesus of being a blasphemer. With this miracle the scribes, the conscience of Israel and experts in the Mosaic Law, had

Jesus heals the man with palsy.

moved from being dangerous critics of Jesus to being malevolent enemies.

We learn of Jesus' power and authority over sin from this miracle account. This is the great good news of the gospel—through Jesus Christ we can be free from the power of sin. Forgiveness of sin is the most fundamental miracle of all, and it is our joy and privilege to share that good news.

Again, we have our model in Jesus when it comes to expressing sympathy and forgiveness. For example, the palsied man in this story heard two words of encouragement and hope from Jesus—his sins were forgiven and he could walk again. People around us in the hurly-burly of life are starved for sympathy, forgiveness, and encouragement. We are to respond to that need with words and actions that point toward a Jesus who cares about their needs and hurts.

The call of Matthew.   At the end of his second cycle of miracle stories Matthew pauses again to talk with us about discipleship. And here the scene shifts as Jesus selects Matthew, a tax collector in the Capernaum customs office, to be one of His disciples (9:9–13).

In calling Matthew to be a member of His inner circle Jesus flouted all that was right and decent to the Jews. Tax collectors were an evil and unscrupulous lot, known for their dishonesty and despised by their fellow countrymen. In addition they were not even permitted to worship in the synagogue. But obviously Jesus saw something in Matthew that prompted His trust. Matthew's response was instantaneous. When Jesus said "Follow me," Matthew left his customs desk and joined the other disciples.

Next we find Jesus enjoying dinner with Matthew and his friends. In doing this Jesus deliberately disregarded tradition and demonstrated His authority over the social prejudices of the scribes and the Pharisees. I don't believe He did this to be contentious or arbitrary, but when Jesus saw people in need, all artificial and superficial religious and social walls had to collapse. It is people who are important, not their vocation.

In response to those who criticized Jesus because He ate with publicans and sinners, He made a bold pronouncement that has brought comfort and hope to millions over the passing centuries, "I will have mercy, and not sacrifice: for I am not come to call the righteous but sinners to repentance."

Here Jesus demonstrates the truth that background and social status are not important. He can use anyone as long as they are fully committed to Him. No one is excluded from His love and care. And we can exclude no one from our love and care.

It is rather interesting at this point in our lesson to see that it wasn't only the Pharisees who were puzzled and affronted by the unorthodox behavior of Jesus and His disciples. John the Baptist's disciples were equally puzzled by their unconventional style—they didn't follow the rules (9:14–17). For example, Jesus' disciples didn't practice fasting as part of their religious observance. Instead they seemed to enjoy life; they weren't slaves to custom.

In response, Jesus likens Himself and His disciples to a bridegroom and his groomsmen. They enjoy each other; it is a happy time when they are together. But then in the fifteenth verse Jesus looks ahead once more and alludes to His coming death when He speaks of the bridegroom being taken away from them.

The parable of the new wine.

To conclude this particular teaching Jesus used the parable of the patched wineskin and the new wine to illustrate His relationship with the old religious patterns of Judaism. We know that Jesus respected Israel's spiritual heritage, but He had come to introduce a new way that transcended the old forms. This was a time for change— the old ways needed to be replaced—not patched.

To pour the new wine of the gospel into the old wineskins of Judaism would be to lose both. Jesus' listeners knew well the analogy—as new wine fermented it would burst old wineskins. Similarly, the new life of Christianity could not be controlled by the old structures.

We have in this parable a vivid illustration of how the church needs forms, but it also needs freedom to change old forms and develop new ones. This doesn't mean that the heart message of the gospel changes, but it must take on new structures as customs and times change. Our minds must be open to the Holy Spirit's guidance, and this requires more than living by rules.

There are vital, practical lessons for us in these teachings of Jesus. Our twentieth century has seen more change than all the previous centuries of human existence. These are exciting times as we move ahead into a new technological age. The world has been reduced to a neighborhood and communication is instant. But while we must constantly search for and use new ways and shapes in our witnessing and living, the redemptive message of the gospel remains unchanged. The principles Jesus gave us for life and wholeness are as right and workable today as they were in the first century.

The Compassionate Shepherd (9:18–38)

In our pilgrimage through this lesson so far we have moved at a breathless pace. We have witnessed six miracles as Jesus has moved across the countryside ministering to the needs of people. Now, in the next twenty-one verses we continue to see Jesus in action as He performs four astounding miracles. Life is restored to a girl that was dead, a woman is healed of a debilitating hemorrhage, sight is restored to two blind men, and a demon-possessed man is healed. What an awesome demonstration of Jesus' power! But as we shall see in each instance, it is the faith of the petitioner that is emphasized and is important.

A miracle within a miracle.

First, Matthew has blended a pair of stories into one narrative to form a miracle within a miracle. Both, however, emphasize the absolute necessity of faith. The woman with the hemorrhage (9:20–22) was cured while Jesus was on his way to raise a girl from the dead (9:18–19, 23–26).

In verses 18 and 19 we are introduced to a desperate Jewish ruler of the synagogue. In telling the same story both Mark and Luke identify him as Jairus. This distraught man rushed up to Jesus and said, "My daughter is even now dead: but come and lay thy hand upon her, *and she shall live*" (italics mine). In response to this father's agony Jesus went to the ruler's home, and even though He was confronted there by an unbelieving and scornful crowd, He took the girl by the hand and returned life to her body.

The disciples must have been thunderstruck. Miracle-working rabbis were no rarity in Judaism, but no one expected the Messiah to raise the dead. Their faith in Jesus' authority must have grown enormously as they watched the girl walk around her house.

But let's double back a moment, for earlier, while they were walking toward the ruler's house, a woman was healed as she reached out and touched the fringe of Jesus' robe. She was ritually "unclean" because she could not get her menstrual period to stop, and according to the Law, a woman in that condition was forbidden to touch anyone. But she approached Jesus in the crowd and secretly touched Him, hoping to not be detected as she violated a strict Jewish law. But in spite of her audacious act Jesus healed her and called her by the affectionate name "daughter."

Next, Jesus was accosted on the street by two blind men (9:27–31). We don't know why Jesus didn't respond to their initial pleas for mercy and help, but they were persistent and followed Him to the house. It was here that Jesus asked them the all-important question, "Believe ye that I am able to do this?" He tested their sincerity by asking them if they thought He could restore their sight. Without hesitation they both said yes. And in response Jesus reached out, touched their eyes, and said, "According to your faith be it unto you." What a poignant moment! The words and the touch of Jesus and their faith combined, and a miracle happened.

Jesus heals two men.

In the final miracle of this awesome series Jesus healed the demon-possessed mute. Matthew's Gospel sharply contrasts the crowd's reaction of marvel and acclaim with the cynical and hateful attitude of the Pharisees (9:32–34). Again they insisted that Jesus' power came from demonic sources: "He casteth out devils through the prince of the devils."

The healing of the demon-possessed mute.

In very special ways three of these miracles stress the necessity of faith for healing. It can be a powerfully strong faith such as Jairus had. After all, Jesus had not raised anyone from the dead before, but Jairus' faith in Him led to a magnificent miracle.

On the other hand, the hemorrhaging woman seems to have had a very tentative faith. There is no indication of boldness or confidence as she quietly followed behind Jesus and touched the fringe of His robe. After all, if nothing happened, no one would know what she had done. But the important thing was that she had made her move.

And the two blind men vividly illustrate the importance of both persistence and faith. The response of Jesus to them—"According to your faith be it unto you"—is a promise we can hang on to. It is as true for us as it was for the two blind men in the story.

Jesus has modeled for us in these four miracle accounts a striking lesson of the kind of compassion and tenderness we are to feel for human need. In our busyness it is so easy to ignore the needs and hurts of others. And so often the response we do make is second-hand—we dish out a few quarters or dollars to salve our consciences. But this is not the pattern Jesus gives us here. When He saw a need, He acted *personally*. He took a detour to go to Jairus' home, and He personally touched the eyes of the blind men. Jesus did not help or heal by proxy; He involved Himself.

In concluding this ninth chapter of his Gospel, Matthew gives us a brief summary of Jesus' activities (9:35–38). He continues teaching, preaching, and healing, and attempts to challenge His disciples with the needs of people. Then, the harvest was great—the opportunities for witnessing and service are still great. Jesus' instructions are clear—we are to act as He did.

Teaching　## When Disciples Become Apostles, 10

The mighty works of Jesus which we have been studying in the eighth and ninth chapters of Matthew are necessary preparation for the tenth chapter. Here Matthew gives us the second of Jesus' five Teachings—it is a manual of practical exercises for Christian witnesses—a mission charge to us to become involved in our work as apostles.

In this chapter we have Jesus' principles for evangelism and mission strategy just as He gave them to His select group of disciples. As witnessing ambassadors of Christ, we are sent by Him and authorized to act as He would act if He were physically present.

Jesus commissions the disciples.

In the opening verses of Chapter 10 Matthew lists the names of the twelve disciples Jesus had selected. They were now ready to be sent throughout Israel as witnesses of the Good News. For months they had lived and learned together; now they were ready to undertake their mission—to "heal the sick, cleanse lepers, raise the dead, and cast out devils." And Jesus gave them the same authority that He had. They were His personal representatives.

In order to get His message to the world and "make disciples of all nations" (28:19), Jesus first sent them to the Jewish communities of Galilee (10:5–15) because they were not yet equipped to witness to gentiles.

The twelve were to do just as Jesus had done—put their faith into action (10:7). Second, they were to confirm their words with mighty acts—healing the sick, cleansing lepers, raising the dead, casting out devils (10:8).

It has always been good for me to remember that these disciples of Jesus were very average men. Yet Jesus trusted them to be His witnesses, and in time their witness and message reached across the world. So often we tend to feel that we don't matter; we're just ordinary people. But as we have seen in our study so far and as we will see later, God uses ordinary people to accomplish extraordinary results —whether it is with the neighbors on our block or with people in other parts of the world.

As Jesus was preparing His disciples for this particular mission, He was careful to tell them they were not to burden themselves with either baggage or money and they were not to benefit financially from their ministry. Instead they were to benefit by the hospitality of their newly won followers. Just as they had freely received, they were to freely give. Their mission was a hurried one, and they were not to be overloaded with other details (10:9–10).

Then in verses 11–15 the disciples received their code-of-conduct while traveling and witnessing. They were to seek friendly people who received them openly. If the people were receptive to their message, the home would receive the blessing of God's grace. But if after hearing the good news of salvation, they chose to remain with the old legalisms of Judaism, then the disciples were instructed to leave. Jesus knew that at times their witness would be rejected.

The disciples' pattern for witnessing.

Jesus also knew that as the disciples moved from place to place in their missionary venture they would encounter hostilities from both the Jewish and Roman authorities (10:16–23). He was very honest in warning them of the difficulties they would encounter. But He also assured them that they would be given the needed resources to meet and handle opposition: "Take no thought how or what ye shall speak: for it shall be given you in that same hour what ye shall speak."

In our daily efforts to serve the Lord we will come up against people who disagree with us, but we are to avoid becoming involved in defensive or hostile exchanges. But what about those times when we can't avoid a confrontation and we must respond? Jesus assures us here that the Holy Spirit will give us the appropriate words to defend ourselves. God will supply us with both the words and courage to handle the time of crisis.

Jesus, our model for witnessing.

Next, in 10:24–25, Jesus shows rare insight in telling the twelve and us that in our witnessing we should remember that He is our model. The teacher is a model for what he teaches—"like teacher, like student." At the same time Jesus warned His disciples that they cannot expect to be treated better than He was. They were to model Him in character; they just might model Him in death, and most of them did.

Jesus knew the paralyzing power of fear, and in verses 26–31 He cautions us to not let fears of any kind cripple our witness in our daily walk with Him. Today we fear competitors; those who disagree with us; tax collectors. We live in fear of nuclear war; we fear the unknown. But the antidote for our fears is the same as Jesus gave His disciples—if God cares about what happens to a lowly sparrow, we need not fear because He cares so much more for us. This is the answer to the paranoia of our time.

As we come to the closing verses in our lesson, Jesus has some important words of counsel and encouragement for us. First, He assures us that if we are faithful to Him, He will be faithful to us. At the same time, unfaithfulness to Him will be punished (10:32–33). Jesus is the great divide between those who know God as a loving Heavenly Father and those who do not. He will acknowledge us if we acknowledge Him.

And second, Jesus tells us that while He came to bring the peace of reconciliation, the result is sometimes estrangement even within our own families (10:34–39). Loyalty to Christ means loving Him more than family, fear of scandal, or preserving our way of life. For first-century gentiles, turning from worshiping the pagan deity Zeus to worshiping Jesus meant possible Roman crucifixion. For Matthew, the central paradox of Christianity is that "he who finds his life will lose it, and he who loses his life for my sake will find it."

Finally, we have the assurance (10:40–42) that even the simplest deed done by us for another person will receive the Lord's recognition. We are all apostles, and every believer is "sent out" by Jesus to be a messenger of the Kingdom. As we—you and I—give our witness for Christ in the twentieth century, we are in the grand tradition of the

twelve disciples as they began to evangelize their neighbors in Galilee about A.D. 30.

Dear Lord, Thank You for Your faithfulness. Help me to become the faithful disciple I should be, and not only that, but to go on and become a faithful apostle.

WHAT THIS SCRIPTURE MEANS TO ME—Matthew 8–10

The messages in these chapters come like the wind, yet they are personal, touching us where we are.

The importance our Lord gives to faith stands out vividly.

The leper, the sick woman, and the blind men had faith in Jesus' power to help them. The centurion, and those who cared for the paralytic, believed He could help their loved ones. By responding warmly and strongly to their faith He encourages us to bring to Him, not only our own needs, but the needs of others.

"I will come (to your servant)," He assured the centurion. "I will come (to your loved one)," He assures us today.

Brigadier General James Dozier, captured by the Red Brigade in Italy in December of 1981, was not expected to escape alive. During his captivity countless hundreds of people prayed for him. After his release he told of having sensed their prayer support.

"When you're on the receiving end of prayer," he said, "you feel it."

Faith opens us to our Lord's power in a special way.

Perhaps as a child, you read the book *The Secret Garden*. In the story a boy and girl find a small secret door that leads into a walled garden. Entering the privacy and beauty of that enchanted spot becomes their chief delight.

Faith is our door in the wall of life. It is to be our response as we move through our own life story.

Several years ago, I went to the home of a close friend whose dearly loved husband had suddenly and unexpectedly passed away. All through the day people came bringing flowers, food, and their sympathy.

Then night came. Everyone had left, the children had gone to bed, and the house became still. We finished cleaning up the dishes, turned off the kitchen lights, and I prepared to leave. But then I thought of the loneliness she had to be feeling. I asked if she would like me to stay with her through the night.

I'll never forget her answer. A person of deep faith, she responded, "Oh, no. You see, I'm not alone."

Because of her belief, there shone a profound peace and strength which only our Lord could have given her.

The "great calm" Jesus impressed on the storm-tossed sea He imparts to us as we turn to Him in faith.

And we are not only to have faith but we are to accept the absolute sovereignty of our Lord. He is to reign in every area of our lives.

One day, while taking a walk, I was silently praying. Feeling very burdened at that time, I complained to God that it seemed there were far too many difficulties in my life. My thoughts, centering on my problems, whirled around in clamoring, anxious confusion.

Suddenly, into the turmoil came two words—simple, profound, clear.

"Follow me."

Did the words shape themselves from my memory of our Lord's words to Matthew, or did He speak directly to my heart as I walked and prayed on that warm summer day?

I don't know, but either way their simple clarity cut through my confusion with authority. The seeming importance of my difficulties faded. What mattered was not the problems, but *following Him in the midst of them.*

To me, some of Jesus' most precious words conclude these chapters. His attention to our small acts of service touch me deeply: a cup of cold water matters. We may not convert thousands or establish a hospital, but the small acts of kindness that mark our days are noted by our Father in heaven.

LESSON 4
MATTHEW 11–13

Jesus Revealed but Rejected

BOOK III

Lord, Increase my understanding. AMEN.

In his third book, Matthew shifts the scene from Jesus commissioning His disciples to doubts, criticisms, and overt hostility about Jesus being the Messiah. Up to that point He had enjoyed rapid and widespread success among the people. But the rumblings in the background now began to take center stage as Jesus concluded His ministry in Galilee. Cities that had welcomed His miracles did not respond to His call to repentance. The derision among His hearers grew sharper until Jesus was rejected in His own headquarters town of Capernaum. Critical voices challenged Jesus at every turn.

The Rejection of Jesus, 11–12   *Narrative*

As we have moved through the Gospel of Matthew, we've observed the varied reactions of the people and the religious leaders to Jesus' teaching, and we have discovered His pattern for effective witnessing and living. But at this point Matthew inserts a warning. Not all who profess an interest in Jesus and His Kingdom are happy about it when He comes. Our initial response may be positive and our first hopes and intentions may be good, but when we

Five Responses to Jesus (11:1–30)

The first response.

begin to see and understand all that is involved in the authentic Christian life, we may decide that the cost is too high and turn our backs on Him.

In the eleventh chapter of Matthew we will look at five responses to Jesus from the people. They run the gamut from cautious acceptance to outright scorn.

The response of John the Baptist comes first. John's response to Jesus' Messianic activity was a mixture of doubt and confidence (11:1–11). John had been arrested by Herod the Tetrarch (ruler) of Galilee and imprisoned in the fortress of Machaerus by the Dead Sea. But apparently he was allowed visits with his disciples, and as they discussed the events of Jesus' ministry, John decided to send two of them to Jesus and ask for "proof of His Messiahship." John had expected a more militant Messiah than Jesus turned out to be, and he was uncertain and confused.

In response to John's instructions his disciples find Jesus and ask Him the crucial question, "Art thou he that should come, or do we look for another?" In reply, Jesus told John that he would find his answer in the prophets. The blind would see and the deaf would hear (Isa. 35:5); the broken-hearted, the meek, the captives, and those in prison would be ministered to and hear the good news (Isa. 61:1). Jesus wanted John to see that what He was doing fulfilled the Old Testament view of the Messiah. It was true that His words and actions brought judgment, but His mission was to heal, cleanse, liberate, and save people. Jesus also wanted him to understand that the Cross of suffering and sacrifice was to become the supreme symbol of Christ's redemption and judgment.

I have always been impressed with the tender and compassionate way Jesus handled this conversation with John's disciples. Jesus understood the background and the thinking that prompted this honest question. But He wanted them and us to see that a true Savior would not cater to our nationalism or to our pride and love of comfort. Instead He would bring a message of love and light and comfort and healing to the spiritually hungry.

A true Savior would not castigate us for infractions of rules or for duties left undone. Instead He would challenge us to be sensitive and open to God's will as we seek to model our lives after the example given us by His teaching and compassion for others.

Matthew's second example of the five responses to Jesus refers to men of violence who wanted the Kingdom to serve their own purposes (11:12–15). Jesus' words here are difficult to understand because we can't be exactly sure which violent men He had in mind. He may have been referring to armed extremists such as the Zealots.

The second response.

But we are two thousand years removed from the Zealots and Roman soldiers and the Pharisees. So we have to ask: What do these verses mean to us now? First, I believe Jesus is telling us that we are not to use our relationship with Him to beat our personal enemies into submission.

We are not to gloat over the defeat of those who differ with us in any way. While we should be enthusiastic Christians, our zeal should be focused on turning the world upside down for goodness and love. Focusing on love does not produce a soft or easy faith but catches the spirit of the Great Commandment: love God; love others.

Matthew's third example of responses to Jesus is seen in the public reaction of fickle displeasure over Jesus' lifestyle (11:16–19). They were fickle in their reactions because on one hand they had criticized John the Baptist for his austere and simple way of life—living in the wilderness, dressing in crude clothing, eating a diet of wild locusts and honey. On the other hand they criticized Jesus because of His free and convivial lifestyle—He enjoyed the company of friends and frequently banqueted with people His critics accused of being sinners. It was a no-win situation.

The third response.

But Jesus' response here is that the results of His ministry will prove His words and actions to be right. Jesus knew that His methods of reaching people were right even though His strategies didn't conform to the ridiculous and rigid rules His critics lived by.

We see from this model just how careful we must be in our criticism of others. We tend to look down on people who don't think and act the way we do, whose lifestyles may be different from ours, who may not worship the way we do. But what really counts is our inner relationship with Christ. It isn't necessarily the outward show that matters, but the inner experience with our Lord.

Matthew next points out the response of flagrant rejec-

The fourth response.

The ruins of the city and synagogue at Chorazin, located about four miles north and east of Capernaum. Chorazin was one of the cities on which Jesus pronounced judgment. This fourth-century synagogue is probably located over where Jesus preached.

tion of Jesus by the people in several cities of Galilee (11:20–24). He specifically speaks of Chorazin, Bethsaida, and Capernaum—all of these were just a few miles apart and within walking distance of each other. It was in this area that Jesus spent a lot of time teaching and healing. The people here knew firsthand who He was and what He did. Yet they were indifferent to the deep meaning of His message.

It is important for us to realize here, though, that Jesus didn't condemn them in a fit of anger because we know that the meaning of "woe" as Jesus used it here connotes heartbroken condemnation. They were guilty of indifference to Christ—the sin of doing nothing. This was apparently the sin of Chorazin, Bethsaida, and Capernaum.

Matthew's fifth example is the model of childlike trust in contrast to the other four (11:25–30). In this prayer (11:25–28) Jesus is equating lowliness and faith. The "wise" and proud scribes and Pharisees rejected Him while the simple, humble common people accepted Him. But the point here is not that Jesus is deprecating cleverness or intelligence. Instead, He is speaking against intellectual and spiritual pride.

The fifth response.

We also learn from the words of Jesus here that it is God who will help us understand the truth about Himself. And we come to understand that truth comes through Jesus Christ—it is not attained through our own intellectual efforts.

We come now in verse 27 to the grand climax of this short prayer. It has been called the spiritual autobiography of Jesus. He knew the Father and the Father knew Him intimately. If we want to know what God is like, then we need to look at what Jesus is like. Only He can help us come to know God as our Heavenly Father. He, Jesus, is the Word that was with God from the beginning (John 1:1).

In verse 28 we find the great Magna Charta of the Bible as Jesus invites us to leave the heavy loads of legalistic religion and come to Him for relief. "Come unto me" is the grand invitation for everyone who is tired and exhausted —tired of carrying a rigid religion that imposes a massive burden of rules.

He then invites us to "Take my yoke," a phrase used by Jewish teachers to invite a person to become their student. But from His years in the carpenter shop Jesus also had to be familiar with the ox yoke. He knew that it had to fit right (easy) if the oxen were to pull together the way they were supposed to.

For us, the invitation is to get rid of the ill-fitting yoke of legalism and slip into the easy, well-fitting yoke of Christ.

In this twelfth chapter of Matthew we find a new level of intensity in the Pharisee's opposition to Jesus as they begin to plot His death. Their resistance becomes vitriolic when they see that Jesus threatens their whole religious system—a system that focuses on religious rites as ends in themselves.

The Liberator versus the Legalists (12:1–50)

For example, the Sabbath had become an object of national pride, and had almost become an idol in its elevation over the needs of the people. When Jesus changed the Sabbath regulations as the scribes understood them, He shook Israel's national emblem to its core. The Pharisees had lost the true spirit of the day and had become nitpickers over what could and could not be done on the Sabbath.

"Remember the sabbath day, to keep it holy" (Ex. 20:8) was the fourth of the Ten Commandments given at Mt. Sinai, and originally the Sabbath was intended as a day of rest, recreation, and worship. The commandment was simply worded, but through the centuries it had accumulated hundreds of scribal prohibitions. For example, thirty-nine major kinds of work were forbidden on the Sabbath. Also forbidden was the boiling of an egg for lunch on the Sabbath.

The conflict in the grain field.

This pathological preoccupation with rules is graphically illustrated by a situation recorded in Chapter 12, verses 1–8. The disciples were hungry as they walked along a path through a grain field on the Sabbath (12:1–8). It seems they picked some of the grain, rubbed it between their hands, blew the chaff from the kernels, and then ate it. What was wrong with that? Plenty! The disciples were guilty of breaking three Sabbath laws; they had reaped, threshed, and winnowed the grain. And the picayune Pharisees were incensed! In typical tattle-tale fashion they ran to Jesus and told Him the disciples had broken the Law.

Next, in rebuking the legalistic criticism of the Pharisees, Jesus gave a new interpretation of the Sabbath that stressed His role as Lord and Liberator of that day. Jesus used two illustrations from the Old Testament Scriptures to attack their legalistic attitude. First, He reminded them that King David, a hero of the Pharisees, had not hesitated to eat the holy shewbread from the Tabernacle when he and his men were hungry (1 Sam. 21:1–6). And He next reminded them that the temple service could not be carried out unless the priest worked on the Sabbath (Num. 28). Certainly, instances such as these completely overshadowed the action of the disciples.

Jesus shocked them by claiming to be Lord of their holy day and greater than their temple (12:6–7). But He did not repudiate either the temple or the Sabbath even though He placed human need above both.

Although the Sabbath day issue may not be a critical one for us, there are some helpful thoughts that we can draw from this confrontation. Even as with Jesus and His disciples, it is inevitable that we will be criticized because of the way we express and live our faith. Unfortunately, tolerance is not the strongest of virtues even in the Christian community. But the important thing is the way we respond to any critical attacks that may come our way.

When Jesus was attacked by the Pharisees on the Sabbath issue, He didn't lash out in anger with thunderous and self-righteous denunciation. Instead, He calmly referred them to their own Scriptures, building His reasoning on David and the practices of the priests in the temple. It seems to me that Jesus' gentle and reasonable approach may have been intended to pacify their anger. Perhaps then, they would listen more closely to the point He wanted to get across. I see in Jesus' attitude a superb model for our own responses to criticism—no one ever scores a point by making the other person angry.

The incident in the grain field was accidental, but controversy in the synagogue was deliberately provoked by Jesus (12:9–14). I believe He intentionally went into "their synagogue" (probably in Capernaum) so He could heal the man with the withered hand on the Sabbath. It is even possible that He already knew the man. But whether Jesus did or did not know him, He was certainly aware of the fact that there was no emergency based on the nature of the deformity. In other words, no damage would be done to this man if Jesus had waited one more day to heal him. But it seems quite likely that He healed the man on the Sabbath in response to the challenge of the Pharisees.

"Is it lawful to heal on the sabbath days?" was nothing more than a catch question. But again Jesus' gentle approach appealed to their reason by suggesting that even the most scrupulous Pharisee would not leave a sheep in a pit until the Sabbath was over. And then He added, "How much then is a man better than a sheep?" Then came the postscript: it is lawful and right to do good on the Sabbath. And with that Jesus completely cured the man's hand.

Again, Jesus' point is well made. People in need are more important than rules—especially those rules that shore up personal bias or gain. The religious leaders of Jesus' time repeatedly revealed their true selves by ignor-

The conflict in the synagogue.

ing people in favor of their regulations and practices. But Jesus undermined their security by being concerned for people who are hurting. His compassion added fuel to their fires of hostility, and the Pharisees eventually plotted amongst themselves "how they might destroy him."

Although Jesus wasn't afraid of the Pharisees, He had to be very careful to avoid being arrested as a "lawbreaker," so He put some "creative distance" between Himself and them (12:15–21). His moral victory was complete, but He withdrew quietly to avoid a premature confrontation.

Matthew uses this paragraph to contrast the gentle ministry of Jesus with the fury of the Pharisees by drawing from the words of Isaiah 42. Jesus stressed fairness and justice, but He didn't do it in a willful, contentious manner. Although authoritative in tone He didn't engage in bitter shouting matches with those who opposed Him. And as Isaiah prophesied, "A bruised reed shall he not break," Jesus was sensitive to those who were discouraged and whose faith was weak.

The ministry and manner of Jesus contrasted sharply with the rigidity and arrogant self-righteousness of the Pharisees, who insisted on their "rights" irrespective of the cost to others.

The conflict with spiritual blindness. In the third of the escalating conflicts, Matthew shows us how ugly judgments grow out of ugly hearts, and while judging Jesus the Pharisees judged themselves (12:22–32). Jesus, out of love, gave a blind man his sight; the Pharisees, out of hate, retreated into further spiritual blindness. The "unpardonable sin" of the Pharisees was to attribute to the devil the good deeds accomplished through the power of the Spirit of God.

In His three temptations in the wilderness immediately after His baptism, Jesus had thwarted Satan, but the conflict raged on during His years of ministry as He continued to upset Satan's plans. When Jesus healed the man who was blind and mute, the crowds were impressed and began to have a tentative faith in His Messiahship. But the Pharisees responded with a contemptuous insult and attributed his healing power to Beelzebub (Beelzebub means "lord of dung").

The term "unpardonable sin" is widely misunderstood, and countless Christians and others have clung to this idea without knowing the original situation where the Pharisees accused Jesus of acting out of evil motives. Once when I was a volunteer counselor in a Billy Graham Crusade, I talked with a young lady who was deeply concerned that she might have committed the unpardonable sin. But, her worry alone was evidence that the Spirit of God was at work in her life and that God was not through with her. Only where the forgiving voice of God cannot get through is a sin unpardonable.

By again accusing Jesus of acting in league with the devil the Pharisees had condemned themselves. And Jesus now held them responsible for their terrible accusation (12:33–37). Out of an ugly heart come ugly words because thoughts reflect character. Words are important. What we say is a reflection of our inner thoughts. We sometimes refer to a "slip of the tongue." More often than not a "slip" isn't involved. How cautious we need to be of both our thoughts and our words!

When the scribes and the Pharisees heard this response of Jesus, they immediately became defensive and demanded a "sign from heaven" to prove He was the Messiah He claimed to be (12:38–42). By now Jesus was using some pretty blunt language because He knew they were baiting Him. Their request for something dramatic and magical was merely a ploy. However Jesus answered their request in the same way He had answered John the Baptist: His actions and words were enough to cause people to trust Him. He reminded them that even as Jonah was a sign of God's love to Ninevah, He was God's sign of love to Israel.

Finally, Jesus concluded his fierce dialogue with the Pharisees with a strange parable (12:43–45). We have here the story of a man who had been freed from an evil spirit. But, unfortunately, nothing filled the vacancy that was left. When the spirit returned and saw this, he went out and located seven other evil spirits and they all took up residence in the man.

The parable of the haunted man.

This is rather a strange story, but it speaks to an important truth. From the time of Ezra to the time of Jesus the Jews had so codified their religion that everything in life was regulated by rules. Although their rules kept them from many of the sins that had plagued people for centuries, they now had an empty and negative religion. It looked good from the outside, but the inside of their spiritual house was empty because nothing positive had been added. God himself needed to come into the house and fill it or the sickness would return even worse than before.

The application of Jesus' story not only spoke to Israel; it has profound truth for us. The presence of evil in our world is a reality. Newspaper and television news remind us daily of the world's sinful condition. But if in our spiritual pilgrimage we are busily working for the Lord, our "house" is full—there isn't room for even the appearance of evil. This calls for diligence and commitment on our part, but the rewards are rich in a deepened fellowship with God and our fellow Christians.

In the final scene in this chapter (12:46–50) Jesus' mother Mary and His brothers came to take Him away from the crowds because they were afraid the Pharisees would lynch Him. We get the impression from this scene that His family thought He had gone out of His mind. Remember, it wasn't until after His resurrection that Jesus' family came to understand Him.

When Jesus was told they were there, He asked a seemingly puzzling question, "Who is my mother? and who are my brethren?" There is no hint here that Jesus was not devoted to Mary and the rest of His family. But He was affirming the extended family God had given Him—His devoted followers then, and all who have committed their lives to Christ over the passing centuries.

It is good to be able to affirm and enjoy our flesh and blood ties. Family and family roots are important. But in Christ we have a great extended family in our Christian brothers and sisters. They need our support, and we need theirs.

When an associate of mine became a Christian, he said, "I lost all my friends." But then he added with a smile, "After about six months God gave me a new set of friends." These were brothers and sisters in Christ! His family circle had expanded way beyond what it was before.

Teaching   ## *Parables of the Kingdom, 13*

As we have so vividly seen, a storm of criticism and hatred has gathered around Jesus since He sent out the twelve as witnesses of the Good News. Matthew's collection of seven parables in this chapter is given against this background of strife. The parables were meant to assure the disciples that, even though some of their labor might seem wasted, there would be an abundant harvest. Through these stories Jesus answered their present rejection with a promise of future victory.

Jesus used parables, which are actually short stories drawn from everyday life, to enlighten His hearers as to the truth He wanted to convey. The honest and sincere person caught the meaning of His stories, but the merely curious or critical usually missed the point. However, the stories were worded carefully to avoid offending those who were hostile or unprepared to receive the truth.

The parable of the Sower.

The purpose of the first parable about the Sower was to encourage the disciples in their witnessing (13:1–9). As we will see in these nine verses, Jesus tells the story; the explanation comes later. He knew that His listeners were very familiar with the scene He was building. It is even possible that within sight of where He was speaking a farmer was actually sowing seed in one of his fields.

This parable makes it clear that the Sower (Jesus) knows His soil (His hearers), and He knows what to expect from it. He understands that alongside most fields there is a walkway (wayside) where some of the seed is bound to fall. Then, too, there are stony places and thorn patches. And, of course, there is good, productive soil.

We see the Sower (Jesus) faithfully sowing the seed of salvation, unconcerned about the stones and the thorns and the walkway—the hostility of the scribes and Pharisees and the increasing indifference of the crowds to His message. But the story ends with the amazing word that the returns from the seed sown in the good soil ranged from a ratio of thirty to one to as high as one hundred to one.

Now, with the completion of the story, Jesus interrupts Himself with an explanation of why He was using parables in His teaching. It is even possible that someone in the crowd questioned Him (13:10–17).

Jesus made it clear that He wasn't trying to hide the truth by teaching in parables. He wanted everyone to understand the truth and find salvation. But He spoke to the crowds in parables because as yet they didn't understand His message, and they had to be challenged to do so. His purpose for telling parables was not primarily to illustrate with stories but to evoke a spiritual response

In the Parable of the Sower Jesus tells about the sower and the different kinds of soil. The seed that fell on good ground produced abundantly. Pictured here is an abundant wheat crop in modern day Israel.

from the crowds. It is as we respond to Christ that we begin to understand the meaning of His message.

Having given His rationale for teaching by telling stories Jesus goes on to explain the parable of the Sower by calling attention to the four types of soil or hearers (13:18–23). He explains that some hearers are indifferent. Some are shallow but respond enthusiastically because they don't yet understand how difficult it may be to follow Jesus. Others have competing ambitions which choke out the claims of Christ. And others welcome the Word and respond gladly to the challenge of the gospel. Jesus then closes His explanation with the assurance that the crop—the results of their witnessing—will be good in spite of the opposition.

This parable encouraged the disciples, even as it heartens us today. Like most people, I tend to be influenced by statistical success or the lack of it. When my witnessing efforts are not received with enthusiasm, I tend to question my effectiveness. But then I remember that my responsibility is only to sow the seed. The results are in God's hands.

Jesus' second parable also talked about seed—two kinds of seed (13:24–30).

The parable of the wheat and the tares.

Jesus plotted His story in a setting His listeners could easily identify with. It is the saga of a conscientious farmer who, after carefully preparing his field, sowed good seed. Then, according to the story, one of the farmer's enemies slipped into the newly planted field at night and sowed some darnel seed. To us this sounds ludicrous, but it wasn't an uncommon occurrence in Jesus' time when a person wanted to get even with an enemy.

Now, darnel was actually a poison weed, but it looked exactly like wheat until the heads formed. By then, though, the thickness of the growth would make it impossible to pull out the darnel (tares) without also pulling out some of the wheat. This is why the farmer in the story refused to let his men pull out the darnel when they discovered what it was. Instead, they left the field undisturbed until harvest time and then they could safely separate the darnel from the wheat—the wheat to be saved and processed and the darnel to be burned.

Fortunately for us, the disciples asked Jesus to explain the meaning of the story. This He does in verses 36–43, and the explanation has profound meaning for us now even as it did for Jesus' listeners. We are cautioned here against hasty judgment of the spiritual integrity of others. There is also a caution against any self-righteous isolation of ourselves from others.

The Pharisees (the "separatists") had been criticizing Jesus because He refused to separate Himself from those who were regarded as sinners. Even John the Baptist had been puzzled because Jesus did not call down the immediate fire of judgment on the wicked. But Jesus insisted that only God could separate the true from the false, and He would not do that until the time of final judgment.

From this story we are further reminded that we should leave any judgment of others to God. He alone knows the hearts of people; He alone is qualified to separate the good from the bad. Also, we have seen in the actions and attitudes of the Pharisees what can happen to us if we are judgmental. Judgmental people are usually harsh, abrasive, and brittle—not pleasant to be around. Their influence is negative on Christians and non-Christians alike, and the effectiveness of their witness is severely hampered.

The parable of the mustard seed.

Jesus' third parable repeats the theme of seed (13:31–32). The mustard seed is one of the smallest of garden seeds, but in Palestine it frequently produced a plant that grew to twelve feet in height. This was a story of encouragement for the disciples, for the early Christians, and for us now. The Jews had expected the Kingdom of God to come with awesome spectacle, not from a little baby born in Bethlehem and reared as a peasant in Nazareth. They wanted military power, not a humble Suffering Servant who taught a gospel of love. But Jesus encouraged the twelve disciples with the truth that the Kingdom of God would far exceed its humble beginnings around the Sea of Galilee. And those same humble beginnings produced a faith that has spread rapidly and influenced the world for almost 2,000 years.

The parable of the leaven.

Jesus paired the parable of the mustard seed with another one that expresses the same theme (13:33). He says the Kingdom of God is like a tiny piece of leaven (yeast) in forty pounds of bread flour. As the dough is kneaded, allowed to stand, and then baked, the leaven does its work and expands the dough into a loaf of bread.

This story illustrates how the Christian message will spread throughout the entire world. It will change everything it touches with revolutionary force—people, social orders, economic relations, and, finally, the course of history. Because of Jesus the world will never be the same again. Our hospitals, colleges and universities, our judicial systems, and our agencies for alleviating human need and suffering are all traceable to the small beginnings of Jesus' ministry in Galilee and Palestine.

It seems to me that these rather homey stories say two things to us. First, they reassure and encourage us in our own service for the Lord. What we do may at times seem so small and insignificant, but we can take heart in knowing that it is part of a vast network of faith across the world.

Second, these stories speak to our penchant for bigness and showmanship in evangelism and witnessing. We have become a "bigness is better" society even in our churches and Christian work. But for the most part throughout history, the gospel has been a quiet revolution as the yeast of Christ's teaching has worked in the hearts of people and through the church. This is not to say that bigness is never effective, but our priorities must be to always "seek first the Kingdom of God."

Again, Matthew appears to interrupt when he adds that in his opinion Jesus used parables not just as illustrations, but to conceal the truth from insincere listeners (13:34–35). After all, if His hearers could not identify with His teaching, they would not identify with any of the people in His parables. Jesus taught to be understood, but the parable method gave His hearers an option to either be a part of or reject His movement.

Jesus now gives us in quick succession two parables which show that the Kingdom of God is worth whatever sacrifice is necessary—it is the best way of life. And the joy that comes from having the best cannot be measured (13:44–46). Both stories challenge the hearer to make a decision to follow Christ.

The parables of the hidden treasure and the expensive pearl.

First, we have the story of the man who accidentally discovered that there was treasure hidden in a certain field. Then Jesus goes on to say that the man so valued the treasure that he sold all of his other assets so he would have money to buy the field.

The second story is about a businessman whose specialty was pearls. One day he found the finest and most costly pearl he had ever seen. Immediately, he liquidated all of his other assets and bought the pearl.

Both of these stories illustrate the inestimable treasure we have in the gospel of Christ. The deep joy and satisfaction that comes to us in our Christian experience is worth any sacrifice.

As in the time of Jesus when He told the Parable of the Dragnet, fishing boats still work the waters of the Sea of Galilee. The boats and equipment are different today, but the results are the same as 2,000 years ago.

The parable of the dragnet.

The parable of the net (13:47–50) (a seine used in fishing) is similar in meaning to the story of the wheat and the tares.

Again, this was a very familiar setting to Jesus' listeners. They knew all about this kind of fishing net—a large, square net with ropes at the corners and weights placed so that when it was hauled by a boat, it would scoop up all the fish in its path. Then when the fishermen pulled the net up to shore, they would separate their catch, selecting only the good fish for market.

Telling the Good News, not making judgments, was the apostolic vocation of the disciples. This was a vital point for the early church even as it is for the church and Christians today. We may not understand or even approve of some who are in the "church net," but we are not to do the sorting or the judging. Remember, even Jesus did not force Judas out of the circle of the twelve. As with the story of the wheat and the tares, we are to leave the separating and the judgments up to God. He alone knows our intention, and He alone understands our deepest longings.

Jesus has now concluded His series of parables about the Kingdom of God, and He says to His disciples, "Have ye understood all these things?" In response to their affirmative answer He holds before them the ideal—a converted scribe who was expert in both the old Law of Moses and the new Law of Christ (13:51–52). It was the ideal of Jewish Christianity to preserve the best of the "old" religion and meld it with the "grace" and power of Christ.

In other words, the knowledge and the gifts that we had before conversion will help us immeasurably in our Christian lifestyle. For the Christian, no knowledge or gift is ever wasted—all is useful in our life for Christ.

Following this teaching series Jesus made a pilgrimage to Nazareth, His hometown (13:53–58). The irony of the homecoming was that Nazareth was the least prepared of all towns in Galilee to understand Him. They knew Him so well externally that they failed to *know* who He really was. After all, they had known His mother and father; they knew His brothers and sisters, and they had known Him as a boy and as a young man in the carpenter shop. They were too familiar with Him to think He was the Son of God. Some were curious, some were jealous, and some showed outright hatred. They were unbelievers because of their familiarity with Him. But Jesus didn't strike out at His hometown folks for rejecting Him, however it must have cut Him deeply to be rejected by His boyhood companions and friends.

Lord Jesus, The more I learn about You, the more I love You. Let the soil of my life be fertile ground from which You can reap an abundant harvest.

WHAT THIS SCRIPTURE MEANS TO ME—Matthew 11–13

As I read the chapters in this lesson, I am reminded of the way I felt as a young girl riding my horse through the fields in springtime. I was filled with wonder and gratitude.

Answering John's question, "Are you he who is to come…?" Jesus responds in a way that gives insight into both His nature and ours. He tells John that His words and works reveal His identity.

He strikes this chord again when He tells His critics, "Wisdom is justified by her deeds." Later He teaches, "The tree is known by its fruits."

Jesus helps us understand that by our words and actions we disclose who we are.

I have found it helpful, and sometimes painfully revealing, to ask myself what my deeds tell about me and my walk with our Lord. I also ask if my words reflect His love and will.

At a luncheon party I attended, several of the guests were talking about a person who was not present. The torrent of criticism exposed the person's apparently abundant failings. Finally, they turned to one of the guests who had not joined the conversation.

"You know her best of all," they said. "Tell us what you think."

"No comment," came her quiet response.

An embarrassed silence fell over the group. Her two words blanketed the fire of cruel gossip, putting it out.

Jesus tells us our words come from "the abundance of the heart." He reminds us that the quality of our thoughts is vital. A lovely Christian teacher, Gertrude De Kock, taught that the thoughts in our minds are like the furnishings in our homes.

She believed that if we are careless, we tend to accumulate discordant, unwanted, and unattractive furniture and bric-a-brac. The result is unpleasant, even depressing. However, should we replace the clutter with carefully chosen pieces that fit together in pleasing harmony, the result can be charming.

In the same way, our minds can gradually accumulate unattractive thoughts such as self-pity, envy, and resentment. Yet with God's help, we can identify, confess, and clear these thoughts out. If we replace them with lovely thoughts, our mind can become a beautiful place filled with kindness, humor, strength, and good will.

Her thought picture has stayed with me for many years.

Our Lord's invitation, "Come unto me, all who labor and are heavy laden," has moved off the pages of the Bible into the hearts of countless millions.

A businessman once told me, "I know of nothing in Scripture that has been of more help to me than those words. They sound the very depths." Remembering an agonizingly difficult period in his business life, he said, "There were times when I felt that those words of Jesus were all I had."

Matthew closes the chapters in our lesson by telling us that Jesus could not do "mighty works...because of their unbelief." Once again comes the call to simple faith and trust in Him.

A friend, Phil, shared with us this story of his childhood. From the time he was born his father signaled him out as a rival. As a boy, he was bewildered and hurt by his father's coldness.

As a young man, Phil was very determined to establish a warm relationship between them. But the father rejected Phil's efforts and built his wall of suspicion and jealousy still higher until finally, before he died, he refused to see Phil at all.

This tragic story reminds me of how our Lord yearns for us to put aside our blocks of unbelief, to open the door to Him who would bring love and fulfillment into our lives.

LESSON 5
MATTHEW 14–18

Life in the Church Community

BOOK IV

Jesus, Help me to see You *in every word of this lesson.* AMEN.

So far in our study we have seen the growing hostility toward Jesus. Now in this fourth Book we see the storm clouds of hatred growing darker. The death of John the Baptist made Jesus wary of falling into the clutches of Herod Antipas, the son of Herod the Great. Since Jesus had openly challenged the guidance the religious leaders of Israel provided, He had to be very careful around the scribes and Pharisees (14–15).

On the brighter side, a little community of faithful believers, which Matthew will later call the church, began to emerge among the twelve disciples (16–17). We will have the opportunity of watching this little group and seeing how it comes to depend upon Jesus for its spiritual food. We will watch as the disciples confess Jesus as the Messiah, and we will stand in awe with them as we see His divine glory revealed in the transfiguration.

In the Teaching section (Chapter 18) we will listen to Jesus lay down the principles on which the little community of believers is to conduct itself both in character and discipline, and we will see the controversy around Jesus grow sharper. This section will prepare us to start with Jesus on His final journey to Jerusalem and the crucifixion which Matthew wrote about in Book V (19:1).

The Founding of the Church, 14–17

Narrative

This section of the Gospel is structured around three rejections and three retreats. First, Herod Antipas threatened Jesus. Then Jesus retreated with His disciples to lay a more secure foundation for the emerging Christian fellowship. Here we see the growing fury of Jesus' enemies on the one hand and the deepening spiritual maturity of the disciples on the other.

Next, the scribes and Pharisees began to close in on Jesus and He left the country with His disciples in a second retreat.

The third retreat (Chapter 16) was the turning point for both Jesus and the disciples as they confessed their belief that He was the Messiah. It was at this time that Jesus told them of His approaching death. The disciples became more of a Christian fellowship, and Jesus steeled Himself for His final showdown with His enemies in Jerusalem. The inner community grew stronger as the outer circumstances deteriorated. The final paradox in Matthew is that we gain our life by losing it.

Rejection and Retreat (14–15)

In His hometown of Nazareth Jesus had felt the warmth of family and lifelong friends turn to cool contempt. Then the government of Herod turned against Him, and He had to escape. John the Baptist had been executed earlier, but Matthew inserted the story of John's death at this point, I believe, to show why Jesus had to retreat from the domain of Herod Antipas (14:1–12). It is believed that Matthew relates John's story as a foreshadowing of Jesus' fate.

The death of John the Baptist.

The death of John the Baptist is a tragic story; a good prophet was sacrificed for a weak man's passions. Herod had stolen his brother's wife Herodias and married her. John had denounced the marriage, and Herod put him into prison to keep him quiet. Herod would have murdered John to silence him, but the prophet was so popular with the people that Herod hesitated to kill him.

At a birthday party for Herod the seductive daughter of Herodias danced for the probably-drunken Herod and his friends. Then as a reward for an erotic performance, Herod offered to give her anything she wanted. The girl ran to her mother for advice, and Herodias told her to ask for the head of John the Baptist. It was delivered on a platter; John was killed without a trial.

Now, when Herod heard of the preaching of Jesus, it reminded him of the preaching of John (14:1–2). His superstition and guilty conscience caused him to wonder if John may have returned from the dead to haunt him. Because of his uneasiness about John's death Herod became a potential threat to Jesus.

Herod may have been weak and foolish, but he was also evil and deadly as a rabid fox. Jesus knew this and decided to leave Herod's jurisdiction by seeking refuge elsewhere (14:13–21). But Jesus hadn't gone far before He was surrounded by a crowd, and in His compassion for the people He hesitated long enough to spend the day healing their sick. When evening came the crowd was still with Him, but they had made no provision for food. The disciples urged Jesus to send the people away so they could buy food, probably at Bethsaida. This set the stage for one of Jesus' most spectacular miracles.

The miracle of the five loaves and two fishes.

In response to the disciple's urging, Jesus amazed them by asking them to feed the crowds. In protest they called His attention to the fact that they had only five barley loaves and two small dried fish. But after instructing the crowd to sit down, Jesus took the meager loaves and fish, blessed them, multiplied them, and gave them to the disciples to distribute. More than five thousand men plus women and children ate their fill, and there was plenty of food left over.

Following the desert supper Jesus quickly sent the disciples away and dismissed the crowd (14:22–33). The Gospel of John tells us why (John 6). Because of this astounding miracle there was a clamor in the crowd to proclaim Jesus as King. But He quickly defused the situation and withdrew into the hills to pray.

The first lesson we learn from the miracle, popularly referred to as "The Feeding of the 5,000," is that when we turn over our little bit to Jesus, He multiplies it and uses it. But we also see something here of the compassion of Jesus. Even though He was weary and wanted to be alone, He set aside His own needs and schedule to minister to needy, hungry people and to heal their illnesses.

Most of us become impatient with interruptions. We become slaves to our schedules. But to Jesus people were more important than schedules. This is a hard lesson for us to learn. I shudder when I think of people who possibly needed my help but didn't receive it because of my preoccupation with a schedule.

Following the feeding of the five thousand Jesus instructed the disciples to return home by boat without Him because He wanted to be alone to pray. Evidently, though, the disciples spent the evening and the early part of the night either on the shore or near it discussing the amazing events of the day and giving vent to their frustration because Jesus refused to play "king." The urge to crown Jesus as Messiah was on the minds of the crowd, and it was still on the minds of the disciples.

But sometime later, possibly around the middle of the night, they started their four-and-one-half-mile boat trip across the corner of the lake. Before they could make it across, however, they were caught in the fury of a storm. Suddenly, off in the distance they saw a figure walking on the water toward them, and not recognizing that it was Jesus, "they cried out for fear."

But then Jesus spoke to them, and in response Peter said in effect, "Lord, if it is really you, ask me to come and meet you on the water." Jesus responded with one word, "Come," and Peter stepped out of the boat and walked on the water toward Him. But as Peter felt the roughness of the water and heard the whistle of the wind, fear gripped his heart and he began to sink. In desperation Peter shouted, "Lord, save me," and immediately Jesus lifted him up by the hand.

The first-century church, especially after it ran into fearful persecution by the Roman government, often turned to this story for comfort. It offered them reassurance that in the midst of life's violent storms Christ is there to deliver, and He does not fail even those who fail Him.

There is a message in this story for those of us in the late twentieth-century church as well. First, we can expect stress and distress in the course of our Christian life and duty; this is a certainty. There is nothing about our discipleship that promises an easy time.

But along with that we can be equally certain that when we need it, help from the Lord is available. He may come to us when we least expect Him, but He will come.

Jesus and Peter walking on water.

Then, too, we learn from this episode that we, like Peter when he stepped boldly out of the boat onto the water, can draw enormous faith resources from God as long as we keep our eyes off of ourselves and our own efforts. But the moment we take our eyes off of Christ and focus on the difficulties nipping at us we will begin to sink. With Peter we take on a boldness and courage in the presence of Christ that we never dreamed was in us before.

Dietrich Bonhoeffer was a German theologian and preacher who was imprisoned by Hitler during World War II. On April 8, 1945 he conducted a Christian worship service for his fellow prisoners with the full knowledge that he had only minutes to live. As soon as he finished the service, the German guards led him to his execution. As he left, he said to a British officer: "This is not the end, but for me it is the beginning of life." For two thousand years Christians have used the story of Peter walking on the water to meet life's most awesome terrors.

Immediately following the episode with Peter on the Sea of Galilee we find Jesus once again in the middle of a crowd of people (14:34–36). The sick and diseased pressed in around Him, and Matthew tells us that *everyone* who touched the fringe of His robe was healed. Everyone in the Galilee region had heard about Jesus and His healing powers, so those with physical disabilities of any kind clamored for His attention. Although Jesus knew that His popularity was based on their superstition, He responded with compassion.

The confrontation over ritual.

Now our lesson takes us into the fifteenth chapter of Matthew where we find a shift in the drama as we are led into the second cycle of rejection and retreat stories.

The religious hierarchy at Jerusalem was convinced that Jesus was a dangerous liberal because, while He observed the pious practices of Judaism, He took strong exception to many of its customs. This infuriated the scribes and Pharisees because they had devoted their lives to the ritual Law, and from their vantage point any deviation from what they considered right and proper should be punished by death. So they traveled all the way north to Galilee in an effort to trap Him into saying or doing something that would give them an opportunity to charge Him with heresy or blasphemy.

This particular confrontation began innocently enough

when they asked Jesus why His disciples did not ritually wash their hands before eating (15:1–20). Actually, this was a minor point, but they were hoping it would lead to something more serious. Jesus could have easily diverted their attack by getting into an endless debate, but instead He responded by accusing them of using the traditions of the elders—the Oral Law—to get around the commandments of God, and He cites their misuse of one of the Ten: "Honor thy father and mother."

The washing of hands was not a rite commanded by the Old Testament Law, but was introduced in later centuries by the scribes and made a part of the "tradition." By the time of Jesus this Oral Law was composed of a horrendous body of customs and possessed equal authority with the written Law (Genesis, Exodus, Leviticus, Numbers, and Deuteronomy). The nit-picking scribes refused to distinguish between the significant and the trivial, so they made everything significant.

Jesus recognized the authority of the Old Testament Scriptures, but He rejected the vast accumulation of oral tradition and its phony marks of piety. In doing so, He refused to make a distinction between the ritually clean and unclean. They accused him of ceremonial uncleanness, and He charged them with moral uncleanness.

We are a long way from being concerned with ceremonial "hand washing," and we certainly understand that purity of life comes from the heart and is not affected by what we eat. But there is a practical message for us today from this story.

We definitely get the impression here that Jesus was disturbed and angry with their question and implied accusation. He knew through their distortion of the commandment to honor and take care of their parents that they were not really concerned about an infraction of rules. We find in His emotional reaction a pattern for us. We cannot casually accept as Christian any attitude or act that circumvents the spirit of Jesus' words. Hypocrisy in any form is an affront to the Christian.

Also Jesus reacted as He did here to their misuse of religion. Their nit-picking preoccupation with rules was evidently driving away the common folk that Jesus most wanted to win. How easy it is to obscure the saving message of the gospel with our "Christian games" of exclusivity or of attacking those who differ from us in any way.

The third thing that disturbed Jesus was that the Pharisees focused on a trivial outer defilement of "unwashed hands" and ignored the evil that was inside the heart. We cannot overcome evil with a list of rules and regulations. Instead, inner defilement can only be handled by a total commitment of our lives to Jesus Christ.

Jesus heals the daughter of the Phoenician woman.

Perhaps to avoid more arguments with the Pharisees, Jesus left Galilee and journeyed west to the gentile region of Tyre and Sidon (15:21–28). Jesus had said earlier in the dispute with the Pharisees that there were no external tests for what is clean or unclean. Now in this episode with the Phoenician woman He demonstrated that there were no distinctions between clean and unclean people, that is, between Jew and non-Jew.

Matthew tells how this gentile woman came wailing to Jesus and begged Him to heal her daughter. This raised a crucial question: the disciples had failed to understand Jesus when He insisted that all foods were clean; would they also fail to see that Jesus regarded all races of people as clean?

At first Jesus did not reply to the pleas of the distraught mother. This may have been His way of testing the disciples to see whether they understood that His message of salvation and healing reached beyond Israel. If so, they failed the test; they wanted to chase her away.

When Jesus did reply, He said that it wasn't fair to throw the children's bread to the little dogs ("puppies," or children's pets). Now, for a Jew to call someone a dog was a supreme insult, and Jesus probably did this to test her faith even further. But hearing His tone of voice and seeing the smile that was likely on His face, the woman seemed to understand.

Not to be outdone and quick of wit herself, she shot back the clever answer that even little dogs got to eat the crumbs that fell from the master's table. Jesus marveled at her faith and healed her daughter. What a contrast her faith was to the scorn of the Pharisees.

Still keeping a wary eye out for Herod and the Pharisees, when Jesus returned to the Galilee region, He remained in gentile territory (15:29–31). It is quite likely they were in Decapolis, a region southeast of the Sea of Galilee, in which there were ten Greek cities populated mostly by gentiles. When Jesus healed their sick as if they were Jews, the gentile crowds praised "the God of Israel." Thanks to the experience with the Phoenician woman, the disciples were apparently outgrowing some of their racial prejudice.

Huge crowds stayed close to Jesus as He performed numerous healings, but after three days apparently almost everyone had run out of food. His compassion then focused on their hunger (15:32–39). Jesus had previously fed five thousand Jews. Now, showing the same empathy for the four thousand hungry gentiles, He took their meager seven loaves of bread and few fishes and fed them all.

From these two stories—the healing of the Phoenician woman's daughter and the miraculous feeding of four thousand gentiles—we have further proof of the inclusiveness of Jesus' message: His mission is to *all* the world.

Jesus Recognized as the Messiah (16–17)

Matthew starts his third cycle of rejection and retreat stories after Jesus left the Decapolis and crossed the Sea of Galilee back into Jewish territory. Here He was confronted with a challenge and a demand from the Pharisees and Sadducees to produce a miracle. They baited Him to give them a sign from heaven that would make them believe in Him without the shadow of a doubt (16:1–12). Jesus refused to take their bait, but before leaving He pointed out that while they were adept at reading many physical signs, they had missed the most important sign of all. By asking for spectacular evidence they merely proved that they did not see the prophecy from their own Scriptures being fulfilled right before their eyes. They ignored His presence and wickedly sought a sign. Their unbelief was a waste of His time so Jesus and the disciples left.

As they were leaving, Jesus warned His disciples to avoid the error of both the Sadducees and the Pharisees—the first were grossly materialistic and the second were steeped in scheming legalism. The former had adapted to the fashion of the times and lost their influence. The latter had become formalists in religion and ended up as hypocrites.

This third retreat of Jesus again took Him out of Galilee into gentile territory. Caesarea Philippi was a town on the southwest slopes of the nine-thousand-foot-high Mount Hermon, about twenty-five miles north of Galilee. This area had long been a center for pagan religion.

Here Jesus asked His disciples a most important question to find out if they were beginning to understand His

It was in the region of these springs at Caesarea Philippi which form the headwaters of the Jordan River where Peter made his great confession of faith in which he affirmed that Jesus was the Christ.

mission. With penetrating directness He asked, "Who do men say that I the Son of man am?" In responding they gave Him the stock answer—some said He was John the Baptist, others said He was Elijah, and still others said He was Jeremiah (16:13–20).

But then Jesus pushed beyond what popular rumor was saying and asked, "But whom say ye that I am?" Peter spoke out and said, "Thou art the Christ, the Son of the living God." This magnificent personal witness of Peter formed the foundation of the church fellowship that was to follow. Our existence and our survival as a church is tied to the resurrection of Christ from the dead, but our beginning as a Christian community is centered around the Jesus of Galilee and the confession of faith of the twelve disciples that Jesus is the Christ.

Peter declares Jesus is the Son of God.

Verse 18 introduces the word "church" into the Gospel story for the first time. In response to Simon Peter's declaration, Jesus gave him the name Peter (meaning "rock") and declared that on this "rock"—Peter's statement of faith—He would build His church. The church's ultimate foundation, of course, is Christ Himself. The Good News of the Gospel is about Christ; it is not about Peter.

Jesus gives Peter his name.

In many ways this is a difficult passage to understand, but I believe that when Jesus pointed to Peter as the "rock" He meant three things. First, the church was built on Peter since he was the leader and spokesman for the twelve disciples. He was the first among equals. Without the nucleus of the disciples the church as a human organism would never have come into existence.

Second, the faith of Peter is the only kind of faith that leads to the recognition that Jesus is the Christ. Without divinely illumined insight, no one sees the Son of God in the Carpenter of Nazareth.

Third, to publicly confess Christ as Peter did is to join the fellowship of believers. Confessing people make up the church and the church is built on just such a testimony as Peter had given. Matthew seems to see Peter as a type for all the early Christians. As we repeat Peter's discoveries, we too join the company of those early believers.

Verse 19 refers to the "keys of the Kingdom of heaven." The teachers of the Jewish Law ordinarily said they had the "keys" that unlocked the Scriptures and were the ones to interpret them. In rabbinical language, to "bind" and to "loose" was to declare certain actions forbidden or permitted according to their understanding of the Law.

Now Jesus took the keys from the traditionalists of the

old Israel and gave them to Peter and his fellow believers in the "new Israel"—the church.

At Caesarea Philippi the disciples correctly identified Jesus, but they were still haunted by the Jewish expectation that the Messiah would somehow defeat the military enemies of Israel and restore the Kingdom of David. The church, however, is built on the redemptive suffering of the Messiah, a "crucified God." Next, Jesus warned the disciples that He would go to Jerusalem, be tortured at the hands of the ruling Sanhedrin (composed of the chief priests, elders and scribes), be put to death, but then be raised the third day. Jesus had not shared this with them before, but now He wanted to prepare them for His death and resurrection (16:21–28).

But as they heard these words, Peter, speaking for the twelve, took Jesus aside and rebuked Him, ". . . this shall not be unto thee." God would never permit such a thing to happen to His Messiah, Peter claimed. Peter meant well, but his words reflected the same temptation as Satan's words did after Jesus' baptism—follow the easy road to popular leadership and reject the way of suffering.

Jesus, with swift severity, turned to Peter and rebuked him as the voice of Satan. In his great declaration shortly before, Peter had spoken with the inspired words of God; now he spoke in the seductive tones of Satan.

In our struggle toward spiritual growth we so often identify with the impetuous Peter. But in this exchange we see Satan rebuked, and we see, too, that Jesus had confidence that Peter would continue to grow in knowledge and wisdom. We also know that Jesus has invested the same kind of hope in us. Jesus assures us through Peter that we too are capable of thinking God's thoughts. Eventually Peter became the "rock" that Jesus saw in him, and so can we.

The way of the fulfilled life.

Now in the closing words of this sixteenth chapter Jesus gives us the great paradox of the Christian faith: "For whosoever will save his life shall lose it: and whosoever will lose his life for my sake shall find it." It is only as we lose our selfish selves that we find our spiritual selves. The "way of the cross" may well be a "way of suffering," but it takes us to life at its fullest in Christ.

On the morning of July 27, 1945, in the bombed-out post-war city of Berlin, Germany, an elderly German couple sat listening to a daily radio broadcast from London. A memorial service was in progress, and they listened with mounting anxiety. The radio voice said, "We are gathered here in the presence of God to make thankful remembrance of the life and work of His servant, Dietrich Bonhoeffer, who gave his life in faith and obedience to His holy Word."

The elderly father and mother clasped hands and wept quietly: they had finally learned the fate of their son, Dietrich Bonhoeffer. Their son had deliberately chosen to oppose Hitler. He could have chosen to cooperate with Hitler, but prior to his pilgrimage of sacrificial decision he had realized that when "Christ calls a man, He bids him come and die." Dietrich denied himself and took up his cross and followed his Lord.

This is not to say that every one of us will die a violent death, but it does mean that the way to life is through death to self and selfishness. To say "no" to selfishness is to say "yes" to the true self that God created us to be. The only life that lasts is one in which our destiny is fulfilled in proper relationship with God.

In the twenty-eighth verse, Jesus, out of His love for the disciples, is seeking to reassure them that they can count on the coming of His Kingdom. His coming death would not be the end, but with His resurrection they would see "the Son of Man coming in His Kingdom."

The transfiguration.

Matthew's Gospel now moves us six days beyond the climactic discussion at Caesarea Philippi. Jesus has taken Peter, James, and John into "a high mountain apart" where they have seen a changed and transfigured Jesus (17:1–13). They saw Jesus as the heavenly Lord when His face for a short time took on a new radiance and even His clothing became white as light.

As they watched in wonder, Moses and Elijah, typifying the Law and the prophets, appeared and spoke to Jesus. Luke (9:31) tells us that Moses and Elijah talked with Jesus about His approaching accomplishment (crucifixion) in Jerusalem.

During these awesome moments Peter was overcome with emotion and wanted to institutionalize the event by building a shrine, but then a voice from a cloud broke in and announced, "This is my beloved Son, in whom I am well pleased; hear ye him." In these few heaven-sent words the disciples were commanded to listen to what Jesus was trying to tell them.

As you can imagine, the disciples were "sore afraid." But Jesus gently calmed their fears and warned them not to speak of this mountaintop experience when they reached the lowlands. They didn't yet know how to interpret what they saw.

In the description Matthew gives us of the transfiguration of Jesus, we, along with Peter, James, and John see, hear, and experience God's awesome affirmation that Jesus is the Savior. At the same time we are reminded that God has come into our world personally in Christ, and our own nature can be transfigured through commitment to Him. We also see that there is no need for us to try to escape from life through some selfish, mystical experience. We are needed "in the valley below" for service, and Jesus is a sufficient guide and friend as we go about the real business of living.

Healing the epileptic boy.

In the meantime, the nine disciples who had remained at the foot of the mountain had tried without success to heal an epileptic boy (17:14–21). When Jesus arrived, the boy's father appealed to Him for help. Again, in response to human suffering, He healed the boy.

Obviously, we don't know all that happened here, but there is enough for us to get the picture. When the disciples asked Jesus why they hadn't been successful in healing the boy, He responded, "Because of your unbelief." They apparently didn't really believe they could do it.

In further response Jesus used a very familiar picture to help them understand. He reminds them of the smallness of a mustard seed and then tells them if they have just that much faith, they can move a mountain. "Removing mountains" was a Jewish expression for pulverizing difficulties, and Jesus used the phrase to tell them and us that our problems can be solved if we have enough faith in God. Martin Luther captured this idea when he said that faith is a living, daring confidence in God's grace and we can stake our lives on it a thousand times.

On the Mount of Transfiguration we witnessed the glory of Jesus. At the foot of the mountain we saw that same glory at work in the healing of the boy and the joy that came to a distraught father. We are then told by Jesus that our faith in Him can remove our mountains of difficul-

Two locations are possible sites for the Transfiguration: Mount Tabor, east of Nazareth a few miles, pictured here, and Mount Hermon which rises north of Caesarea Philippi. It was on "a high mountain apart."

ties and given the promise that "nothing shall be impossible unto you." This is the God we worship and the Savior we serve.

Next, for the second time, Jesus told His disciples that He would be executed and the third day He would be raised from the dead (17:22–23). From the Mount of Transfiguration Jesus and the disciples had slipped back into Galilee to prepare for the trip to Jerusalem to celebrate the Passover. Here Jesus is still attempting to prepare them for what He knew would happen, but this time He alerted them that He would be betrayed.

The disciples were greatly distressed at this second warning, but at least they didn't rebuke Him as they had a few weeks earlier at Caesarea Philippi. Jesus often tried to prepare the disciples for His rejection, but they were terribly unready for His death. They didn't understand His words about the resurrection. In spite of all that had happened to them and all they had seen and heard in the previous weeks they were still insensitive to what Jesus was trying to tell them. So often we hear and see only what we want to.

Jesus pays the tax.

Jesus now moves on to His headquarters in Capernaum. Here we see Peter as he is confronted by the tax collectors who assumed that since Jesus had so obviously rejected the Law, He would no longer pay the trivial half-shekel tax required of Jewish men for temple upkeep (17:24–27). Immediately Peter denied the charge that Jesus was a tax-dodger, and then hurried into the house to locate Him and find out for certain.

In response to Peter's question Jesus affirmed their liberation from such Jewish customs, but rather than offend the very Jews they were trying to reach, He said they would pay the tax. In high good humor He sent Peter out to catch a fish which He said would have a coin in its mouth that could be used to pay the tax. In this episode we find an important lesson—love sets the limits of our freedom.

Teaching

The Preservation of the Church's Unity, 18

In the Narrative section just studied we saw the beginnings of the church. Now in this Teaching section Jesus tells us about the character of the Christian community.

Just before Jesus leaves Capernaum for Jerusalem He lays down rules of grace for the church He is bringing into existence. The emphasis is on new relationships among Christians made possible by their new relationship to Christ. Ethical qualities are stressed: acceptance of Christians who are of a different background or outlook; providing an example by good conduct and loving generosity; the recovery of weaker members of the church when they wander from the flock; forgiveness of a fellow Christian who may have wronged you; and reconciliation when bad feelings are about to break up the fellowship. Truly converted people lead a new life of greatness wherever two or three are gathered in His name. Christians not only *go* to church, but primarily Christians *are* the church.

The people of Jesus' day were preoccupied with rank and titles. They measured a person's worth by fame, earthly possessions, or victories. This may well have motivated the disciples when they asked Jesus, "Who is the greatest in the Kingdom of heaven?" (18:1–4). Ignoring the idea of rank or title Jesus responded by placing a child, an example of humility, in the middle of their circle and told them that unless they had a childlike spirit they could not even enter the Kingdom.

Life in the Church: True Greatness (18:1–35)

When we are converted, we start life over again. We have a new direction, a new set of attitudes. Jesus is reminding us here that children have a special way of seeing the world that all of us need to learn.

Becoming as "little children."

When Jesus said that we should "become as little children," what did He mean? These are some of the qualities I believe He was referring to: a child is innocent, dependent, and trusting; honest and devoted to the truth; friendly; and unconscious of social rank or race. A child lives in constant wonder and expects great things—and finds them—at every turn. The birthright of Christians is to live each day on tiptoe and with a sense of wonder.

The terms "little child" and "little ones" (18:5,6) can also refer to new Christians. We are being cautioned in these verses against doing or saying anything that would be a stumbling block to those who are young in the faith (18:5–9). It is our responsibility to model Christian maturity for the "little ones" in the faith, and above all, we are not to do anything that would cause someone else to stumble and sin.

Jesus' words in these verses are strong, and He warns of severe judgment if we fail to assume our proper responsibility. This applies equally to the church, for it is through this fellowship that we learn to grow and serve.

Now, building on His statements in the previous verses Jesus reminds us that everybody is important (18:10–14). We are not to look down on anyone irrespective of their cultural background or vocation—whether they are experienced or unseasoned Christians. It is in this context that Jesus gives us that remarkable and well-known parable of

We are all important to God.

the lost sheep. This story describes a picture that isn't particularly familiar to most of us, but Jesus' listeners in first-century Palestine would have sparked immediately to His imagery. Sheep frequently wandered away from the flock in the hills. The conscientious shepherd faithfully searched them out.

For me, the punch line in the story comes as Jesus emphasizes the great joy of the shepherd when he has located the lost sheep. God really cares. In John 3:16 we read that God loves the whole world. But as this parable points out so graphically, He also loves us one by one.

It is so easy for us to be distracted by institutional programs. The work of the church is important. But even as the Palestinian shepherd would leave the flock to go after the one wandering and lost sheep, our first interest must be in people in need.

Forgiving and being forgiven.

Even as Jesus in the parable of the lost sheep gave us a model for our concern about the one in need or lost, He now turns His attention to relationships. Inevitably, ruptures will occur between brothers and sisters in Christ. But in this part of our lesson Jesus gently and wisely describes how we are to act when that happens. Uppermost in our minds must always be that even as God has so readily forgiven us, we are to be willing to forgive others. But Jesus knew that we would need guidance on how to handle stressed relationships, so in 18:15–20 He carefully outlined four steps for us to take.

To set the stage, let's suppose that Arthur, a fellow Christian, has deliberately lied about me. What am I to do? Jesus tells us here that my first step is to go to Arthur alone, tell him what I've heard, and then discuss the problem. This is to be done privately and without fanfare. My manner is to be forthright and open, not abrasive or accusatory, and my purpose is not to put Arthur on the spot or humiliate him but to bring healing to our relationship. And my attitude is to be one of concern about Arthur and his needs rather than the issue that has come between us.

If Arthur and I resolve the difficulty, the matter can be dropped. But if he is hostile and rejects my efforts at understanding and reconciliation, I am then to take several other Christians with me and try again to work things out. These concerned Christians become witnesses to the conversation and can make sure I am being fair and open with Arthur and am sensitive to his feelings and needs.

However, Jesus then says, "And if he shall neglect to hear them, tell it to the church." In other words, if Arthur is still not willing to resolve the problem and be reconciled, then we are to take our differences to a fellowship of believers. In this setting Arthur is to be reminded of his commitment to Christ, and shown lovingly that he must have integrity about the truth if he is to be an effective witness to the unbelieving world outside the church fellowship. At the same time Arthur and I need to be reconciled.

But what if Arthur still refuses to right the wrong after all these efforts? Sadly, nothing more can be done. He is left to live with his own sin, and his fellowship with Christian believers and the church is severely damaged. Arthur has excluded himself from the fellowship by his refusal to do his part in healing the difference.

But we are never to consider Arthur as lost to the cause of Christ. We are to gently seek to win him back by our witness of God's love and forgiveness; no one is to be given up as a lost cause.

It may seem that these words of Jesus demand too much of us. This kind of caring about our relationship with a Christian brother or sister seems unrealistic in practical terms. But God is able to give us grace even for that.

Jesus then went on in verses 19–20 to promise that when ". . . two of you shall agree on earth as touching any thing that they shall ask, it shall be done for them of my Father which is in heaven," and that ". . . where two or three are gathered together in my name, there am I in the midst of them." This doesn't mean that we will arbitrarily get anything we ask for by merely joining with another person in prayer. Rather, the reference here is to what is good from God's perspective for the entire fellowship of believers. The promise is that God does answer our prayers, but He answers them in line with His eternal purposes—not ours. Our action together must conform to Jesus' teachings.

But the grand promise which Jesus gives us here has been of consolation to millions of Christians over the centuries: when we are together in Christian fellowship, Jesus Christ is there with us. With that confidence we can witness boldly to His caring love and forgiving spirit.

Christian fellowship guarantees Christ's presence.

Unlimited forgiveness.   But that's not the end of the story. Peter had quite obviously been listening carefully to Jesus. The message about the need to have a forgiving spirit had evidently gotten through to him. Now he asks a crucial question, "Lord, how oft shall my brother sin against me, and I forgive him? till seven times?" (18:21–35).

Peter's question was a good one. Under the rules of Judaism they were to forgive an offending person three times. Now Peter more than doubled that in his question, but that wasn't good enough for Jesus, "...until seventy times seven"—an infinite number of times. Grace has no limits. God's forgiveness of us is endless—we can do no less for others.

Then, as He did so often, Jesus illustrates His point with a story. In this parable of the "unforgiving slave" Jesus deliberately painted an absurd picture to drive home the importance of our forgiving one another in the church fellowship (18:23–35). With grim humor Jesus told of one man's debt of twelve million dollars (in our currency) and another man's debt of twenty dollars—the one being more than 500,000 times greater than the other.

According to the story, the creditor (king) demanded that the servant who owed him the outrageous amount of twelve million dollars pay up. When he couldn't, the creditor insisted that the servant, his family, and everything he owned be sold in payment of the debt. But the servant pleaded for mercy, and the creditor, "moved with compassion," forgave the debt.

Next we see this same servant demanding payment on a twenty dollar debt from one of his fellow servants. When the second servant couldn't pay up, the first one had him thrown into prison. When the king heard about this, he was furious. After all, the first servant had been forgiven his debt—out of the same kind of compassion he should have forgiven his brother servant.

Peter's question—and ours—was answered. We are to forgive as we have been forgiven. Thomas Jefferson and John Adams were good friends. But as they struggled to bring the United States into existence, they had vigorous disagreements, and in time their friendship was totally severed. After ten years and the mediating efforts of a mutual friend they started writing letters to each other. In his first letter Adams wrote, "You and I ought not to die until we have explained ourselves to each other." The 158 letters they exchanged are a classic repertoire of American history. Both men died on July 4, 1826, hundreds of miles apart, but they had been reconciled to each other.

This Teaching section in our lesson stresses Jesus' insistence on forgiveness and reconciliation. Forgiveness is not a law, but a disposition of the heart which we learn from Christ Himself. In his novel, *Love Is Eternal*, Irving Stone has Mary Todd, the grieving widow of the just slain Abraham Lincoln, say that she cannot forgive the assassin. Her son Tad responds, "If Pa had lived, he would have forgiven the man who shot him. Pa forgave everybody."

Dear God, Thank You for the truths I learned in this lesson. I am challenged to be humble; but the world exalts greatness. I am commanded to forgive everyone who assaults me; but the world advocates retribution. Lord, Your Kingdom makes a radical statement of love on this earth; help me dare to be part of Your Way.

WHAT THIS SCRIPTURE MEANS TO ME—Matthew 14–18

I saw a necklace fashioned of jewels of warm and glowing colors recently. Our lesson contains its own special kinds of varied jewels that strike our attention and enrich our lives.

To me, the great truth revealed in the two accounts of the feeding of the multitudes is not that on a certain day several thousand people were miraculously fed. Rather, it is that the power of Christ can touch and transform the real difficulties of life.

A layman friend felt called, late in his career, to study for the ministry. However, the required three years in seminary presented considerable financial problems for him and his wife.

In much the same spirit as the loaves and fishes were offered to Jesus in the Gospel stories, this couple dedicated their limited resources to the Lord.

After completing seminary and entering the ministry, he reflected with wonder, "That we were able to live happily and comfortably, not wanting or even wishing for more, on a third of my former income, was in fact a miracle."

As our Lord came to the disciples on the storm tossed sea, He comes to help us in our troubles.

A divorced, middle-aged woman who had children to raise was ill-equipped for the job market. She looked at the winds of her adversity and, like Peter, began to sink. Also like Peter, she cried out to the Savior.

His help came increasingly through church, friends, prayer, and Scripture. She was empowered and strengthened and gradually overcame her many difficulties.

"We are never alone," wrote Bishop Everett Jones in his book *Getting Life Into Perspective.* "There is forever a Hand stretched out to hold our own."

Jesus' question to His disciples, "Whom say ye that I am?" touches us as well.

A few mornings ago, I was working on this section in Matthew. It was cold and rainy and our beagle dog was restless. He kept wanting to be let in and out. Each excursion involved his muddy paws scratching on the door and tracking up the floors.

Finally, my patience snapped. I jumped up from my chair and, in a stream of irritation, gave him a piece of my mind.

He lay back down, looking chastened, his ears pressed flat against his head. I returned to my desk and resumed reading where I had left off…"Whom say ye that I am?"

The words seemed alive, directed at me.

"You are the Lord," I whispered quietly…and then, "You are love."

I looked over at our beagle, the innocent recipient of my annoyed outburst, and if my ears had been as long as his, they too would have been pressed flat against my head. I went over to make amends.

In the transfiguration, the disciples witnessed Christ in His glory. How can such an event relate to us today?

Bishop Jones tells of a dedicated nurse he knew about whom there was almost a visible light.

I remember a minister at our church when I was a child. His face shone with the love of God.

As even the smallest raindrop sparkles with the sun's reflected radiance, we can catch intimations of His glory in those who have opened their hearts to our Lord.

Our lesson ends with the section on forgiving. When we have been deeply hurt, how difficult it is to follow Jesus' call to "forgive from your hearts." We can do it only with His help.

Perhaps this is a fitting conclusion to our chapters as through them, over and over, we are reminded of the transforming, enabling power of Christ.

LESSON 6
MATTHEW 19—22

Concerning Judgment

BOOK V

Savior, Let me feel Your Presence as I study this lesson. AMEN.

We see in Matthew's fifth and last Book, which we will study in Lessons 6 and 7, a definite urgency as Jesus moves quickly toward Jerusalem. He leaves Galilee and moves toward the Holy City to make a final appeal to Israel's religious leaders to accept Him as the Messiah.

In chapters 19–20 Jesus challenges the accredited authorities of the religious establishment by His teachings. He exposes the roots of human conduct and makes demands about divorce, celibacy, children, money, and the rewards of discipleship.

In chapters 21–22 we will watch Him appear dramatically in Jerusalem, claiming in lowly majesty and purifying wrath the allegiance due the Messiah. We will listen as He debates the leaders about authority and obedience before denouncing them with tremendous power.

In chapters 23–25 we will hear Jesus soundly condemn Jerusalem and give us a glimpse of what to expect in the time before He returns at the End of the Age. We will see Israel's leaders judging Jesus, but Matthew tells us that in reality they were being judged by God. When Jesus enters Jerusalem, we will see Him implement a series of judgments which will not end until the final Judgment at the close of history.

These seven chapters of our lesson form a tremendous

climax that takes us right up to the crucifixion of Jesus. Judgment is the main theme.

Narrative

Jesus Goes to Jerusalem, 19–22

Demands of Discipleship on the Way (19–20)

Jesus and divorce.

As we begin this lesson, we find Jesus leaving Galilee and moving south in the region east of the Jordan River and heading for Jerusalem (19:1–15). Along the way a sharpshooting squad of Pharisees are on the prowl to set a trap for Him by asking a trick question about divorce, "Is it lawful for a man to put away his wife for any cause?" The last three words "for any cause" were crucial. All rabbis granted divorce, but the school of Rabbi Hillel permitted a Jewish husband to divorce his wife for nearly any cause. This lax school of thought even allowed divorce if the husband became attracted to a woman who was prettier than his present wife.

On the other hand, the strict school of Rabbi Shammai insisted that legal divorce was allowable only if the wife (or betrothed) was unchaste. But neither of these two groups authorized the wife to divorce the husband since a woman was considered her husband's property. Jesus' debate with the Pharisees seems a world away from the social mores of our own century, but we can still learn from this exchange as Jesus explains God's plan for a lasting marriage.

Jesus had already discussed marriage and divorce in the Sermon on the Mount (5:31), and He had stressed then the terrible injustice that could be committed against an innocent wife. In these verses (19:3–9) Jesus points to the guilt of a husband who remarries after divorcing a wife who is innocent of any wrongdoing. Remember, the first-century world was man-centered. Jesus, by insisting that wives be respected, was trying to protect the rights of women who could easily be victimized.

In responding to their question Jesus avoided the Pharisees' clever trap. He explained God's intention for the home at the creation of the world—the life union of a husband and wife in a covenant relationship. God made man and woman complementary in nature and intended them to become "one flesh" (or "personality"). "What therefore God hath joined together, let not man put asunder."

The Pharisees responded to Jesus by turning immediately to the Law. They claimed that Moses the great Lawgiver commanded divorce (Deut. 24:1). Jesus answered by saying that Moses did not command divorce but permitted a compromise because of the sinful nature of the people. But the certificate of divorce in Moses' time did protect the woman a little, for if she remarried, at least the first husband could not accuse the second husband of stealing his property. Jesus, though, declared Himself firmly against the practice of divorce for the wrong reasons. By His words He sanctified marriage as a lasting relationship.

Winston Churchill, at a banquet given in his honor, was asked who he would choose to be, excluding himself, if he were given another life to live. Looking at his wife Clemmie and smiling, he quickly replied, "I would choose to be Mrs. Churchill's second husband." This seems to me to catch the spirit of what Jesus meant by lifelong relationships. In any case, Jesus contradicted the Pharisees here in emphasizing the permanence of marriage. God wants a stable family life, and divorce is not part of His original purpose.

Unity in marriage is a creative act of God in which a man and woman can find fulfillment. To break the unity of the home is to do schizophrenic injury to it. When the family, the basic unit of our society, becomes hurt, then our entire social structure suffers.

As we move along, though, to verses 10 through 15, it is fascinating to see how the disciples exposed their own social conditioning when they observed that it might be better not to marry at all if it wasn't possible to dissolve the relationship except when the wife was unfaithful. They didn't mention the possibility of a wife getting trapped with a bad husband. Neither did they mention that success in marriage depends on *being* the right person as much as *finding* the right person.

When the disciples introduced the idea of celibacy, Jesus said it was a matter of personal decision. In God's original creation marriage was to be the pattern, but some disciples might choose celibacy in order to be more involved in their work for God. However, the single disciple should not feel superior to the married disciple, or vice versa.

Jesus not only sanctioned marriage in the scene described in verses 13–15, but He also blessed children. This is a heartwarming scene. Two things seem to stand out. First, in spite of the actions of His disciples Jesus reached out warmly to these little children. He saw in them the honesty, openness, and trust that are so important to a walk in faith. Second, it seems here that the children were attracted to Jesus. They were drawn to Him, and He made time for them.

Jesus and the rich young ruler.

Matthew continues with his account of Jesus' teaching by telling us the story of a rich young ruler who asked Him, "Good Master, what good thing shall I do, that I may have eternal life?" (19:16–30). The young man evidently believed that eternal life could be earned, but Jesus explained that goodness was found in God alone and not in anything he could do. Then as now, goodness is what we are; it expresses itself in what we do.

To discover this young man's true motives, Jesus challenged him to keep the commandments. He was immediately assured that the young man was already doing this. Jesus then had the opportunity to strike at the heart of the young man's problem, and He said, ". . . go and sell that thou hast, and give to the poor."

Jesus had perceived that the young man idolized his money and material possessions above everything else. He hadn't learned the lesson that prosperity was a tool to be used, not a deity to be worshiped. Matthew now tells us that this injunction was more than the young man could handle, for "he went away sorrowful."

Probably most of us studying this lesson would say that we don't have a "wealth problem." But compared to countless millions of people across the world, we are wealthy. I began to realize this when I started traveling regularly in Middle Eastern countries. Seeing myself through the eyes of those people, it dawned on me just how wealthy I was. It was then that I began to sense that my *attitude* toward wealth may be more important than the actual amount of cash I have. So I came back to this story of the rich man and asked myself, "What went wrong with him?"

First, I suspect that making money and acquiring material goods had top priority in his life. His problem wasn't that he had money but that it was more important to him than anything else. His values were misplaced. It may well have been true, as he said, that he had been faithful in keeping the Law, but he hadn't been keeping the spirit of the Law.

It is possible, too, that this young man had fallen prey to the "security syndrome" that most of us are familiar with. We place our confidence in what *we* can do. The rich young ruler in the story asked, "What good thing shall I do?" While we may not put it quite that way, we so often act as if our security depends on what *we* can achieve. We easily lose sight of the truth that our eternal life is a gift from God—this is our true security.

Third, this young man was probably so busy keeping the rules—"All these things have I kept from my youth up"—that he didn't have concern or compassion for people in need. But in His reply Jesus underscored the truth that any idol that demands our loyalty must be destroyed. Everything we are and have must be surrendered to the will of God.

All of this was too much for the young man in the story. Matthew tells us "he went away sorrowful." What a tragic waste!

Turning from that scene to His disciples, Jesus used one of His great hyperboles when He said that it would be easier for a camel to walk through the eye of a sewing needle than for a "rich man to enter into the kingdom of God." To this the amazed disciples asked, "Who then can be saved?" Then came the classic reply, "With men this is impossible; but with God all things are possible."

It is important for us to see that nowhere in this discussion did Jesus indicate that it is impossible for a wealthy person to be saved. Rather, the danger and the sin comes when money, power, position, vocation, or anything else takes first place over Jesus Christ in our lives.

All of this was very puzzling to Peter. In effect he asked Jesus: We've left everything to follow you. What do we get for it? Peter was like Louis XIV who, upon hearing the news of the French defeat at Malplaquet, asked, "Has God forgotten all I have done for Him?"

In this exchange Peter showed some of the spirit of the wealthy young man, but Jesus kindly assured him that God is generous. We cannot outgive God. For us as Christians all earthly values are reversed, and the values we receive from God exceed anything we have given up. But Jesus also warned that anyone consumed with thoughts of rewards will receive the smallest reward.

To further answer Peter's question and to reemphasize the "first last and the last first" saying, Jesus told the story of a generous farmer (20:1–6). In the story, we see that the rich farmer bargained with workers hired at six in the

The parable of the generous farmer.

117

morning. Then at 9:00 A.M., 3:00 P.M., and 5:00 P.M. he hired more workers who didn't bargain but went to work in trust. At six o'clock in the evening the farmer paid them all a full twelve hours' wages.

The workers who had started at six in the morning grumbled at the farmer's generosity and wanted to revise the wage scale by getting a bonus. But the farmer defended his right to be generous to those he had hired later.

This story gives us a beautiful illustration of the grace and goodness of God. We do not deserve His blessing, and we can't earn it. God gives 100 percent to everyone who asks in faith irrespective of the time in life that we come to Him.

The last trip to Jerusalem.

The scene shifts now. The trip south from Galilee is about over. For the third time Jesus warns His disciples that execution awaits Him in Jerusalem (20:17–19). But this time He included a note of horror and humiliation—He would be betrayed, turned over to the gentile Romans to be mocked, scourged, and crucified. Then He added, "And the third day he shall rise again." But the disciples were so absorbed in their own selfish ambitions that they didn't get the message about His death or His resurrection.

The disciples' ambition.

We do get a clue, though, as to what was on the minds of some of them, for Matthew next paints a picture of their gross ambition. Evidently, James and John had been plotting for preferred positions in Christ's Kingdom; their mother had requested special attention for them (20:20–28). They didn't yet see that Jesus' throne would be a cross and that there would be a cross on both His right and left sides when He died.

In response to James and John, Jesus told them they didn't know what they were asking. Then turning to them He asked, "Are ye able to drink of the cup that I shall drink of, and to be baptized with the baptism that I am baptized with?" Their glib answer indicated how unready they were. Then Jesus informed them that not even God could play favorites since greatness in the Kingdom was measured by sacrificial service.

Ironically, both James and John slunk off into hiding like cowards when Jesus was arrested. And at His crucifixion two robbers occupied the left- and right-hand positions.

T. S. Eliot once said that most of the trouble in the world is caused by people who want to be important. But Jesus made His point. It was the voluntary servant ("the last") who would be greatest ("the first") in the Kingdom. Only the Father knew who would occupy those positions.

There is a threefold warning here for us as modern disciples of Jesus. First, we can believe in Jesus and still misunderstand His purposes. We may be estimating Him by our own inadequate standards.

Second, in our rash self-confidence we may exaggerate our powers to do the work of Christ. Our prayers may become flippant and thoughtless due to false pride. We need always to pray for a clearer vision of God's purpose.

And third, thrones are for the Christlike. By the time we are fit for special consideration our motive will no longer be to occupy right-hand or left-hand positions.

At the close of the Revolutionary War the American soldiers, angry that congress was insensitive to their needs, wanted to set up a monarchy and make George Washington king. He pleaded with them to be patient with the democratic process, but they weren't listening to him. To reassure them he took out a heartening letter from a congressman. Before reading it, though, he startled them by putting on a pair of glasses. "Gentlemen," he said, "you will permit me to put on my spectacles, for I have not only grown gray but almost blind in the service of my country." Many of the soldiers wept as they realized the extent of his sacrificial service, and they decided to put their faith in their democratic government.

Our role as disciples of the Lord is to serve Him sacrificially. We have both the teachings and the example of Jesus to follow as our guide.

By this time their travels had taken them to Jericho, just eighteen miles outside of Jerusalem. As they were ready to leave that ancient city, two blind men called out to Jesus (20:29–34). Undoubtedly, they knew that Jesus was coming, and they had surely heard how He healed the sick and restored sight to the blind. They waited in faith— what little they had—and refused to be discouraged, though the crowd around Jesus tried to quiet them. In response to their call for help, Jesus asked them what they wanted Him to do for them, and they responded, "Lord that our eyes may be opened." With a word, Jesus healed them. What a contrast we see here between the twelve ambitious, self-seeking disciples and the two blind men in desperate need!

The Presentation of the Gentle King in Jerusalem, 21–22

The drama now moves with breathtaking speed. Jesus leaves Jericho with His quarreling disciples and enters Jerusalem as a victorious Messiah (21:1–11). But His is a peaceful advance; He is not a political revolutionary. He moves into the city as a humble man riding on an ass, not as a proud warrior on a rearing horse. He is a spiritual leader, not a destroyer of Rome's occupying forces. Still He receives a festive "red carpet" reception from the crowds.

The Triumphal Entry into Jerusalem.

The Triumphal Entry, as we call it today, took place on Sunday morning of Passion Week when the city was filled with Jewish pilgrims from many countries who were attending the Passover celebration. The jubilant crowds gave Jesus the reception of a king, laying down garments in His path and spreading tree branches along the roadway. As He rode along, they shouted, "Hosanna to the Son of David," and words from Psalm 118:26, "Blessed is he that cometh in the name of the Lord." When the foreign pilgrims who were in Jerusalem to celebrate Passover asked who He was, they were told that He was the prophet from Nazareth.

For centuries Christians have celebrated Palm Sunday as a pageant of both royalty and death. It is not a joyous Sunday, but a token of the blindness of human nature to the ways of God. For we know that any modern day city would treat Him with the same set of half-beliefs that met Him when He entered Jerusalem. Our crowds today would be both rejoicing and fickle if He rode into our city, and there is no guarantee that people today would not eventually act as shamefully as they did that week in Jerusalem.

The cleansing of the temple.

Jesus' next move was ominous. Alone and without weapons, but with His own supreme authority, He entered the temple and drove out all who were buying and selling (21:12–17).

Now, it is important to know what was going on here. Jesus wasn't being petulant and provocative. He was outraged at the way sacred observances were being perverted, especially under the direction of the Sadducees. For example, a temple tax had to be paid each year in a specified currency. Jews, especially those from other coun-

A view of the Mount of Olives from the Old City of Jerusalem. It was down the slopes of this hill that Jesus rode on the day of His Triumphal Entry into Jerusalem.

tries, had to exchange their money into the designated currency. But the exchangers abused this practice by charging exorbitant fees for the exchanges. As for the men who sold doves for the sacrifice, they were charging a much higher fee for doves sold in the temple as compared to those sold outside. But the catch was that the sacrificial birds had to be "without blemish," and it was common practice to rule that only those bought inside the temple—in the Court of the Gentiles—measured up. So in today's terms the money changers and the dove sellers in the Court of the Gentiles had a good racket going. It was this profiting from the abuse of their religious practices that Jesus protested against.

Jesus' actions in the temple that day brought immediate repercussions as the most powerful forces in Judaism joined ranks against Him. It was this challenge to the Sadducees who controlled the temple, rather than the Triumphant Entry, that sealed His fate. In this scene we see a Jesus who could not tolerate a religion that preyed on innocent people under a cloak of piety.

The temptation to commercialize the gospel for selfish reasons has plagued the church since its beginnings. Our churches, like the temple in Jesus' day, are meant to be places of prayer, worship, and instruction—places where we meet God and fellowship with other Christians. To turn them into performance centers with show business razzle-dazzle, or to make them places of personal power is a desecration of Sadduceean proportions.

Then, too, in their preoccupation with temple worship and the following of rules there was little concern for what was going on outside, and there was certainly no vision of a world in need. Jesus was revolted at their callous disregard for people except as means to an end.

Similarly, it is dreadfully easy for us to become comfortable and self-contained in our church life. Our world vision becomes blurred or we respond out of guilt with a few dollars for the welfare of "the heathen." But we go to all lengths to avoid becoming personally involved.

William Carey, the British Baptist who eventually founded the modern missionary movement among Protestant Christians, longed for his church to send a missionary to India. But he was sternly rebuked by a Baptist leader who told him, "Young man, if God wants to save the heathen He will do it without your help or mine." Fortunately, Carey would not listen to this selfish reproof, and ultimately *he* responded to God's call and became a missionary to India.

The useless fig tree. Following the dramatic confrontation in the temple, Jesus and the disciples walked the short distance out to Bethany where they spent the night. But the next morning, Monday, as they headed back toward Jerusalem, Jesus saw a fig tree with leaves but no fig buds (21:18–22). The tree was barren, and Jesus was disappointed in it. Looking at the useless tree, He said, "Let no fruit grow on thee henceforward forever." Matthew then tells us that shortly the tree withered away.

This scene at the fig tree gives us a picture of the spiritual condition of Israel at that time. While there was the appearance of life, spiritual vitality was missing—there were leaves but no fruit. The Jewish nation, as the chosen people of God, were supposed to represent Him to the world, but now they were at the point of rejecting Jesus as the Messiah. Jesus had come to Jerusalem (the fig tree) seeking the fruits of repentance, but found none.

Meanwhile, back at the fig tree, we read that the disciples "marveled" at what had happened. They were so impressed with what Jesus had done that they missed the point He was trying to get across. So Jesus quickly changed the subject to faith. He told them that with faith they could move every mountain of difficulty and through believing prayer they would not fail in their work for God. Through prayer they could produce fruit (results).

Jesus' authority questioned.

When Jesus arrived back at the temple that day, the Jewish religious leaders challenged His right to act and teach as He did. "By what authority doest thou these things? and who gave thee this authority?" (21:23–27).

Jesus wasn't ready to answer their question so He outwitted them by asking them a question about John the Baptist. Did John's message come from God or not?

This created a dilemma for them. If they said that John's baptism and authority came from God, Jesus would indict them for not accepting John's endorsement of Him as the Savior of the world. But if they denied that John's authority came from God, the people, who believed John was a true prophet, would be angry with them.

Under the circumstances the only possible answer for them was "We don't know." It was a cop-out, a cowardly answer, and it exposed their insincerity. Jesus responded, "Neither tell I you by what authority I do these things." The debate ended in a draw.

The parable of two sons.

Jesus ended the hiatus of the moment by telling three parables. In the first story (21:28–32), a man asked one of his sons to work in his vineyard. At first the son refused, but later he was sorry and went to work. The father then also asked his second son to go to work. That son agreed, but backed out and didn't do any work.

Jesus asked the authorities which son had obeyed the father, and they answered that the first one had been obedient. The point was clear. The first son represented the very people these Jewish leaders despised—the tax collectors and sinners. While they hadn't professed anything, when they heard the message of John the Baptist and Jesus, they responded in obedience.

He then compared the actions of the second son to the Jewish religious leaders to whom He was speaking. They had promised to do God's will but didn't because of their unbelief.

This story, I believe, makes two points that are important for us. We may at first respond disobediently to God's will and purpose for us. But then, as we recognize our sin and are sorry for it, we move ahead and obey the voice of the Lord. With that, our past is forgiven.

The next point is illustrated by the second son. There is an ever-present danger of making a loud profession of our faith, and then failing to put feet to those professions and daily act out God's will for our lives. This story shows us that past failures won't keep us out of God's Kingdom provided we are obedient from then on. And "lip service" alone is not enough for us to be acceptable to the Lord.

The parable of the wicked tenants.

In His second parable, which was related to the first one, Jesus told the story of a man who planted a vineyard, equipped it, and then went abroad on a trip. The vineyard was left in the care of tenants who agreed to pay their rent from a part of the yearly crop of fruit (21:33–46). At the proper time the owner sent some of his servants to collect the rent money. But instead of paying the rent the tenants savagely attacked the servants. One servant was beaten, one was stoned, and one was actually killed.

The owner then sent a second delegation of servants and they were treated the same way. Finally the owner sent his son to collect what was due him, thinking the son would be respected. But the tenants murdered the son.

Jesus turned now and asked them what they thought the owner should do to the wicked tenants. They responded that the owner should "destroy those wicked men" and get trustworthy tenants. As with the parable of the two sons, the religious leaders had condemned themselves with their own words.

Again Jesus had cast His story in a setting very familiar

to the culture of His time, and Matthew tells us they understood that He was talking about them and their treatment of Him. But at the same time there is meaning here for us.

Jesus knew the attitude and spirit of His listeners. They were in a murderous mood. His boldness and bravery is indeed a model for us in our Christian witness. He understood the intentions of His opposition, but He was faithful to His message in spite of their mood. And He was right, for only three days later they had Him arrested.

Then, too, there is a message for us about the generosity and patience of God. Over the three and one-half years of His earthly ministry Jesus had patiently tried to help the Jewish religious leaders understand who He was. Again and again through His words and actions He tried to win them to the Good News of God's New-Day. And His patience with them reminds us of His longsuffering with us.

This story illustrates the sacrifice that Jesus made. He was the unique Son of the Father, and yet He, like the son of the vineyard owner, deliberately made the trip to our world to give us another chance. The price for our salvation was His life, but it is through His death that we have eternal life.

In His third parable in this series Jesus exposed the spiritual indifference of the religious leaders while foreshadowing the final refusal of the gospel by the people of Israel and the growing movement of the gentile Christians in the plan of God (22:1–14). The story is about a king who planned a wedding feast for his son only to have the invited guests refuse to come.

The parable of the wedding feast.

Later, when the banquet was ready, the king sent another invitation to the same guests asking them to come to the celebration. Most of them made excuses for not going, but some actually killed the servants who had brought them their invitations. When the king heard about the killings, he sent his army after the murderers and killed them. The king then sent his servants to gather guests a third time—they were to go out into the alleys and streets and bring in everyone they could find. This time the banquet hall was filled.

During the feast the king noticed that one of the guests was not dressed appropriately in a clean, white wedding garment. The man, when questioned, had no excuse for wearing a dirty garment, so the king had him removed from the banquet hall.

When Jesus told this story, He was addressing Himself to the Jewish religious leaders who had long been looking forward to receiving an "invitation to God's banquet table" when the Messiah came. But when Jesus did present Himself as the Messiah, they were either indifferent or hostile to Him.

Whether or not Jesus' critics got the point of the parable may be open to question. But from our perspective it is clear. After being rejected twice by his original guests (the Jews), the king then invited all kinds of people (the gentiles) to the wedding. This, of course, foreshadows the apostles' missionary movement to the gentiles of Asia Minor and Europe. And the wedding guest in the soiled garment speaks to us of the necessity of being appropriately prepared to fulfill our role in the Kingdom of God. Good works, a strict following of rules, or even the right language aren't enough to make us acceptable to God. These are as soiled garments, completely out of keeping with the occasion. Such carelessness implies a presence in body but not in heart. The gospel is a call for wholehearted and joyful involvement.

I'm so glad that Jesus used the marriage feast as a picture of what it is like to be a Christian. There is a radiance and joy about being with our Lord that cannot be mistaken. A visitor to New York City tells about taking a walk in Central Park one Sunday morning after he had attended a short church service. He noticed that many of the people he met looked fretful and overburdened with care while others appeared cynical and arrogant.

Later he met a stream of people who looked at ease and relaxed, as if everything in their lives was under control. As he listened to their conversation, he realized that these people had just left a service at the Fifth Avenue Presbyterian Church where Dr. J. H. Jowett was then pastor.

The contrast in appearance and attitude of those who had been in church and those who hadn't was very obvious. Joy marks the true lifestyle of a follower of Jesus.

Two attempted entrapments.

In the telling of the three parables we have just studied, Jesus was on the offensive with His arguments and pronouncements. His words had been a bitter pill for the Jewish authorities to swallow. Now they moved in to counterattack, "Then went the Pharisees, and took council how they might entangle him in his talk" (22:15–22). Next we see them in league with the Herodians in their attempt to embarrass and discredit Him. This was an unholy alliance if there ever was one. The Pharisees and Herod's bureaucrats were natural enemies. But they saw a common enemy in Jesus and made a temporary pact of peace to combine their efforts against Him.

The Herodians were in favor of the Jews paying the annual poll tax to Caesar. But the Pharisees were opposed to paying it for two reasons. First, it was a symbol of foreign tyranny. Second, the tribute coin that was used to pay the tax smacked of the idolatry forbidden in the Second Commandment because it carried on it the image of Caesar.

After these two groups had plotted together, they approached Jesus with ingratiating words of flattery before they sprang the question, "Is it lawful to pay taxes to Caesar, or not?" Immediately, Jesus saw through their ploy and called them hypocrites. He then asked them to show Him the coin stamped with the emperor's profile that was used to pay the poll tax.

When they brought it to Him, He asked, "Whose is this image and superscription?" They answered, "Caesar's." With that He defused their attack completely by saying, "Render therefore unto Caesar the things which are Caesar's; and unto God the things that are God's." In other words, if the Jews enjoyed the benefits of government, they should help pay for it, but at the same time the poll tax should remind them of the greater debt they owed to God. Christians are to pray *for* Caesar, but never *to* Caesar.

In this incident Jesus laid down the principle for us that as believers in Him we have no right to deny the state its just claims, but our loyalty to God must come first. As Christians we have joint membership in our nation and in our Father's Kingdom. In whatever country we hold citizenship we need to give clear witness that we are first-class citizens in both kingdoms, and as such we are to be involved in the problems of our government and society.

Jesus' reply stopped the Pharisees cold: "When they heard these words, they marveled, and left him, and went their way." But later that same day the Sadducees sprang their trap in an open scoff at the doctrine of the resurrection of the dead (22:23–33). They tried to discredit Jesus by telling a hypothetical story of a hardy and enduring woman—

a stock anecdote they had often used with great success against the Pharisees who believed in the resurrection.

According to the old custom of Levirate marriage (Deut. 25:5–10) it was considered the duty of a man, if his brother died childless, to marry his widow. Suppose, the Sadducees said, that a woman following the teaching of Moses in Deuteronomy, had become the wife of seven brothers because each had died without leaving children—whose wife would she be if there was a resurrection?

Jesus' answer to their absurd question (29–32) was amazingly simple and straightforward. But He started out by playfully chiding them for not knowing even their own Scriptures or God's power. Then He went on to explain that it is a mistake to think of the future, eternal world in terms of the present one because the world to come is spiritual in nature.

Next He said that in the resurrection "they neither marry, nor are given in marriage." He reminded them that God is a God of the living, not the dead. Since the Sadducees accepted only the five books of Moses, the Pentateuch, as sacred, He quoted the words of Exodus 3:6 to show that even after Abraham, Isaac, and Jacob were dead they were in spiritual communion with God.

How foolish we are about speculations on the nature of our life to come! It's enough to rest comfortably in the fact of the future of life beyond the grave, for Jesus assured us that He was going to prepare a place for us.

Jesus and the great commandment.

While Jesus was muzzling the Sadducees, the Pharisees regrouped for another attack (22:34–40). One of their spokesmen (a scribe trained in the Law) asked Him a question designed to trick Him into blasphemy, "Teacher, which is the great commandment in the Law?"

Jesus surprised the scribe by responding with not one, but two commandments. The two were opposite in theory but one in practice, thus solving the relationship between the Law and the prophets and exceeding the righteousness of the scribes and Pharisees.

In answering, Jesus quoted the *Shema*, the Jewish confession of faith (Deut. 6:5), that is repeated daily by devout Jews. It demands love for God with all one's being. Then He quoted another verse (Lev. 19:18) demanding that we love our neighbor as we love ourselves. By coupling the two commandments Jesus showed us how to place love over the Law. We love our neighbor by first loving God, and we love God by loving our neighbor. And by loving God, loving our neighbor, and having a healthy attitude toward ourselves, we fulfill all of God's commandments.

This truth in a nutshell is a vivid summary of our Christian duty—to relate to God for His glory and to our fellow humans for their good. And Jesus gets the commands in proper order: our first relationship is to God from whom we learn the purpose of life and get the power to fulfill it. We are to love God with everything—our emotions, personality, and intellect through the open door of Christ. When we properly love God, we can care adequately for other people. For it is only as we begin to truly understand how God has loved us in Christ, that we can know how to truly love our neighbors.

A missionary in India was approached by an aged Punjab Christian who had once been an illiterate and desperate character in the lowest of the caste social systems of that country. He said, "Sahib, teach me some geography." "Why?" the missionary asked. "What do you want with geography at your age?" He replied, "I wish to study geography so that I may know more about who to pray for." This elderly Indian had caught something of the vision of Christ about loving-kindness and improving our relationships with others in a world of oppression, suspicion, and faulty communications.

Having been badgered repeatedly by the religious leaders, Jesus now turned the tables. He fired a question at them that silenced their attacks and brought into focus the basic question about His own identity, "What think ye of Christ? whose son is he?" (22:41–46). This was a purely Jewish argument, and Jesus met His opponents on their own ground. Their response was: "The son of David." Then in verse 44 Jesus quoted Psalm 110:1 and asked how David, the inspired psalmist, could use the divine Name "my Lord" of Him if He was no more than David's son. Thus, Jesus indicated that the Old Testament Scriptures suggest that the Messiah must be more than merely the son of Israel's military hero.

The upshot of the exchange was that the Christ (or Messiah) was not to be equated with David's political career. The son of David could also be the Suffering Servant of Isaiah 53, a man of peace and reconciliation.

Jesus asks the important question.

It is clear that the Pharisees' concept of the Messiah was too limited, for He could be the human descendant of David and also the transcendent Lord—truly man and truly God at the same time.

As truly man, Jesus fully understands our humanity—with its joys, hardships, and temptations. As the divine Lord, He is the *creator* and *source* of our salvation. He comes to us from the Father's right hand of sovereignty with the power to deliver us from spiritual darkness. The Eternal God was in Jesus reconciling us to Himself.

Matthew then tells us that "no man was able to answer him a word." Jesus had answered all of His opponents' questions, but they could not answer a single one of His. As Christians who have seen the truth in Jesus, it is no surprise to us that His enemies withdrew in silence and confusion.

Savior, Help me to live the lesson I've just completed. Let not what I've learned slip away easily from me.

WHAT THIS SCRIPTURE MEANS TO ME—Matthew 19–22

Many of us share the experience of having left a musical show with a particular melody playing in our minds. Like a strain of memorable music, one theme from our lesson returns to me over and over. Humility, Jesus seems to be telling us, is beautiful, important, and necessary.

The disciples tried to send away the children who had been brought to Jesus. One can imagine the restless crowd, the parents' and disciples' voices raised in argument.

How tenderly Jesus' words fall upon the scene, turning the world's values upside down.

"Suffer little children…to come unto me: for of such is the kingdom of heaven."

A little child is the personification of humility. He has no special accomplishments and no real power over anyone.

Robert Frost wrote a lovely poem, *Directive*, which reminds me of this teaching of Jesus. In the poem he tells of children whose playhouse is a pine tree, their toys some broken dishes. He calls his readers to move into a child's simple gladness.

A teenaged girl experienced just this in her own life story. She grew up in a strong-willed, aggressive, and highly competitive family. From her environment she picked up the message that to be an acceptable person she must become a success—outstanding in society, sports, or academics.

However, as time passed, the victories she gained seemed empty and the pressures to excel unrelenting. Depressed and frustrated, she turned to her church and Scripture for help.

One day, while reading her Bible, Jesus' words concerning little children flooded like sunlight into her soul.

She could come to our Lord simply, as a child. He asked for nothing more.

Set free from her burden to excel, her true self, so long suppressed, began to emerge. Her gifts in art and in loving others slowly surfaced. And a sweet joy in creation came forth from her like flowers in a spring garden.

The Kingdom of Heaven truly can be compared to a wedding feast, a reason for joy. Our Lord knows well the way to our fulfillment and highest good.

The mother of James and John came to Jesus desiring positions of importance for her sons. Jesus' response once again rings the theme of humility.

"Whosoever," He declared, "will be great among you, let him be your minister …your servant….even as the Son of man came not to be ministered unto but to minister…"

There is a young woman whose job in a Texas cafeteria involves serving tea and coffee from a wheeled cart as she moves among the tables.

Over the years, she has transformed her task with a remarkable spirit of loving helpfulness. Each person receives with their drink, cheery words, smiles, and personal concern.

She so won the hearts of her many hundreds of customers that she was named Grand Marshall of her town's annual parade, riding at the front with all flags flying.

But her place in the parade was only a symbol of the high esteem in which so many hold her. Her warm, cheerful spirit of service to others is an inspiration to all who know her.

Our lesson repeatedly reminds me that through humility in love and service to God and people we find our greatest fulfillment.

LESSON 7
MATTHEW 23–25

Divine Judgment

Heavenly Father, Reveal Yourself to me as I read about Your love.
AMEN.

Teaching

In this last Teaching section Matthew has assembled and organized the sayings of Jesus on the theme of divine judgment. It begins with an indictment of Pharisaism's pride and hypocrisy and concludes with a powerful scenario of the Last Judgment—when Christ returns to pronounce the ultimate doom of all unbelievers.

We will find a note of sternness and even hostility running through the chapters in this lesson. For those of us who have religious freedom in the Western democracies, it is difficult to picture the first-century Christians' stress, pain, and persecution which occasioned Jesus' strong words of judgment. But as we try to understand what is being said here, we are reminded of our Christian brothers and sisters in many Third World countries, eastern Europe, and Asia, who today endure psychological and physical suffering for their faith. They can understand better than we Jesus' shattering denunciation of spiritual pride and hypocrisy.

A Warning against False Piety, (23:1–39).

Let's turn now to these verses in the first part of our lesson. As far as we can tell, it was still Tuesday and Jesus was yet teaching in the temple area. Earlier that day He had decisively routed the religious leaders in several fierce debates as the scribes and Pharisees tried to trap Him with hypocritical questions. Now He unmasked them as false leaders and bad examples not to be imitated by the crowds or the disciples.

At the time of Jesus, the Pharisees were a group of about six thousand laymen who had devoted their lives to preserving the rules established by their experts in the Law, the scribes. They were typical of Jewish leadership and represented Israel as a whole. While it is true that Jesus agreed with many of their beliefs, He faulted them for not practicing what they preached (23:1–12). Jesus respected the Law, but He warned the people against following the example of the Pharisees. In the third verse of this chapter Jesus tells His listeners that when they teach reverence for God and respect for men, they are to be listened to, but when they turn religion into an intolerable legalistic burden, they are to be disregarded.

Jesus' approach here raises a good question for us: As Christians, how far should we comply with established customs in thinking and acting? Our Lord's example should be our inspired guide—His attitude toward the Pharisees was based on wise conformity to their good traditions and actions, yet He opposed them when He felt they were wrong.

A four point indictment.

In these verses Jesus indicts the Pharisees and their religious leadership on four counts, and at the same time He encourages us not to follow their pattern. First, He says they were heartless (23:4). They placed heavy burdens on the people with their endless rules, and their primary concern was to preserve a religious system. The warning for us is obvious. Our mission offers freedom from tyranny of all kinds. Our primary concern is not to create a religious system or a denominational structure, or to load people down with endless rules.

Second, the Pharisees were guilty of displaying their piety only when an admiring audience was present (23:5). They had an insatiable passion to be noticed and recognized. Quite a contrast to Madame Curie, co-discoverer of radium. Her daughter said of her, "She never knew how to be famous."

Third, they jockeyed for seats and positions of prominence (23:6). In today's world they would have elbowed others to one side for a front seat on the platform of an evangelistic crusade, played politics to become a chairperson of a denominational or church committee. The Pharisees were power brokers. Their striving for position was to manipulate, not to serve.

In verses 8–10 Jesus specifically warns us not to get caught in the Pharisaic trap. As Christians we are not to scramble for position or title. We are all brothers and sisters together in the body of Christ—fellow servants of God. We are to edify each other in the faith. God is our Teacher, and Christ is our Master.

In verses 11–12 Jesus once again raised the issue of what makes us great. As He had said before (in 20:27), the badge of Christian greatness is humble service. The graces of character that Christ covets for us are the opposites of the sins that He had just condemned the Pharisees for.

Seven accusations against the Pharisees.

Now we return to listen to Jesus level seven accusations against the Pharisees (23:13–36), both against their teachings (23:13–22) and against their oppressive legalism in daily life (23:23–36). Each charge is preceded by the words "Woe unto you." The word "woe," however, expresses less a fierce denunciation and more a feeling of grief and compassionate sorrow over their hypocrisy. Jesus always spoke out of love, never out of hate. He intended His words to be redemptive. The seven woes stand in stark contrast to the seven "blessings" of the Beatitudes in the Sermon on the Mount which we as Christians receive.

Jesus directs His first woe (23:13–14) against the hypocrisy of the scribes and Pharisees who were playing a role in Jewish religious observance. Through their concern with the *minutiae* of Judaism they locked the door to God because their actions were not motivated by an inner spirituality. Their repeated emphasis on external acts at the expense of a change of heart was a constant concern of Jesus as we have seen before in His other references to their behavior.

There can be no doubt that this Pharisaical attitude threatened the early church at the time Matthew wrote this Gospel, even as it has plagued the Christian community down to the present time. We, too, can erroneously exalt the letter and neglect the spirit of our relationship to Christ—we can avoid the heresy of form but commit the heresy of spirit. We can, by being exclusive, keep others out of the Kingdom.

The second woe of Jesus is directed to those religious leaders who were attempting to make their gentile converts slaves to their pharisaic pattern (23:15). Many gentiles, impressed with the monotheism and high moral standards of Judaism, were converted and became full members of the Jewish community. These proselytes (newcomers) were the special targets of pharisaic activity, and in their zeal they outdid their teachers.

A narrow religion with a supposed monopoly on God is no model for us to follow. Our witness is to a God who in Christ is reconciling the *whole* world unto Himself—no one is excluded from God's love. The church fellowship is larger than any one Christian or denominational group.

Jesus directs His third woe against the practice of false swearing (insincere oaths) which the scribes had elevated into the science of evasion (23:16–22). They misrepresented the nature of God with their hair-splitting distinctions as to which oaths were binding. The scribes held that oaths sworn by the temple, for example, were not binding, while those sworn by the gold decorations on the temple were valid.

This kind of deception was first discussed by Jesus in the Sermon on the Mount (5:33–37) where Jesus declared that simple honesty is more important than the swearing of oaths. We are not to hide behind equivocal words and actions in our relationships with other people.

The fourth woe speaks against the scribes' and Pharisees' legalism in daily life and their preoccupation with trifles (23:23–24). They didn't understand God's will when they magnified trivia and minimized justice, mercy, and faith. The Jews were instructed in their Law to pay tithes (Lev. 27–30; Deut. 14:23), but they now carried this to ridiculous extremes, losing the spirit of returning a tenth to God. Jesus characterized these actions by the humorous metaphor of their straining wine through cloth to keep out a tiny, unclean gnat, and then turning right around and swallowing a giant, unclean camel.

In these verses Jesus doesn't condemn observance of the Law if its essentials are preserved. Some people have such structured personalities that they take ascetic delight in dealing with trivia, and there is no harm in this. It is only as we fail to give proper attention to the more important that we run directly into the censure of Jesus. We can so easily miss the essentials of being a Christian when our primary focus is on ritual and outward acts and we neglect the spirit of Christ.

The fifth woe builds on the earlier woes. Here Jesus charges the scribes and Pharisees with disregarding their inner sins while giving careful attention to external rituals (23:25–26). The Pharisees revered the "washing of cups and plates," but they made a ceremonial distinction between the cleanliness of the inside and the outside of a cup or plate. They preserved the outward convention of external correctness but neglected the inner purity of the heart. Jesus makes it quite clear that inner renewal and outer life must go together.

The setting for the sixth woe was very familiar to Jesus' audience (23:27–28). The Jews of Jesus' day whitewashed every tomb the month before the Passover celebration so the tombs would be clearly visible and more easily avoided. You see, according to their Law, to touch a tomb was to become sacramentally defiled.

The imagery here is clear. The scribes and Pharisees might be acceptable on the outside, but they were decay and moral ugliness on the inside.

The righteousness that Jesus wants from us far surpasses mere conventional respectability. We can be "respectable" by keeping our sins hidden from public view. I recall gathering hickory nuts as a boy. I would examine each one as I picked it up to make sure it looked good. Then weeks and months later we would find little holes in many of the nuts and upon cracking them discover that the nut meat was all gone.

When I asked what had happened to the nut meat, I was told that tiny insects had drilled holes in the nuts and laid their eggs. As the months passed, those tiny eggs produced hungry worms that ate the nut kernels—then, those worms ate holes in the shells to escape their prison.

I came to see this process of nature as a vivid illustration of the point Jesus was making here. Unless we are inwardly cleansed by the Spirit of God our sinful thoughts and attitudes can silently work down inside until we are destroyed outwardly.

In the last and seventh woe Jesus accuses the scribes and Pharisees of imitating the murderous traits of their spiritual forefathers since they were already plotting to kill Him (23:29–33). Outwardly, they venerated the prophets their forefathers had killed, but their own evil intentions were clear. They were quite prepared to eliminate any contemporary prophet who stood in their way. Our caution here is to not so worship our religious heritage that we become insensitive to our spiritual life and witness today. We cannot live off of the faith of our fathers. Ours must be a living witness of God at work in our lives today.

The cost of rejecting Jesus.

In the closing verses of the twenty-third chapter of Matthew, Jesus gives a stark picture of what will happen because of the scribes and Pharisees rejection of the spirit of the earlier prophets and of Him. He looks ahead with a heavy heart to the terror that would come to Jerusalem in A.D. 70, when the Roman soldiers would destroy the city and the magnificent temple which had been the center of their worship.

In all of this we catch a glimpse of both the patience and love of God. It is not His will that anyone should perish. But, as with the Jewish leaders of Jesus' day, the choice is ours to accept or reject Him. Even as His love and patience is certain, so is His judgment.

Judgment Now and in the Future (24:1–35)

When Jesus had finished His denunciation of the scribes and Pharisees, He left the temple (24:1–2). At some point though, as He was leaving the temple area, His disciples met Him and called attention to the temple building. It was one of the splendors of the ancient world, covering some thirteen acres. The massive white marble building seemed indestructable, but Jesus warned them that the time was coming when it would be leveled— "There shall not be left here one stone upon another."

Startled, and with their attention riveted on Jesus again, the disciples asked Him three questions: first, when would the temple be destroyed; second, what would be the sign of the culmination of His Messianic mission; and third, what would be the sign of the end of the age.

We would have expected Jesus to answer their questions in order by saying, "First, the temple will fall in A.D. 70; second, I will complete my mission by being crucified this Friday and raised from the dead on Sunday; and third, the end of the age is hundreds (thousands) of years in the future."

Instead, Jesus warned them not to confuse the coming destruction of the temple with the final judgment at the end of history. These would be two separate events—Jerusalem would soon be "left desolate," but the end of the world was in the more distant future. Then, instead of taking up their first question, He turned to their last question and began to talk about the signs that would precede the End (24:4–14).

Signs of the end of time.

Jesus told them that there would be three clusters of signs that would take place before the End. First, He warned of false Messiahs (24:4–5)—calamity mongers who would have inflated egos and lead many astray and even to their death, as Jim Jones did in Guyana.

Second, He warned them that nations would go to war against each other and natural calamities would add to the horror of man's self-destruction (24:6–8). It is certainly true that war seems to plague our world. It has been reported that in the last 3,421 years of recorded history only 268 of those years have been free of war. Jesus tells us we are not to be "alarmed." We are to look beyond these military and national convulsions to the redemption that awaits us in the future. Finally, He warned them there would be a time of suffering before the End would come (24:9–14). But those who are loyal followers of Christ will enter into the joy of God's Kingdom.

In verse 14 Jesus tells us that the gospel will reach every nation. The worldwide ministry of Christian evangelism must take place before that Last Day. He made it clear to the disciples and us that God in His mercy wants every person to hear His Good News.

The destruction of Jerusalem.

Jesus then turned to their first question and looked ahead with them to the coming destruction of Jerusalem (24:15–28).

Jesus warned the disciples that there would be a horrible event associated with the temple. This would be a sign for Christians to get out of Judea at once and hide in the mountains. Fortunately, those early believers took Jesus seriously, and they were ready for the Jewish-Roman war when it came.

When the Roman general Titus laid seige to Jerusalem, he unleashed forces that set in motion one of civilization's worst horror stories of starvation and torture. When the

A view of the Western Wall or "Wailing Wall" in Jerusalem. This is all that remains of the magnificent temple of Jesus' day. Jesus predicted its total destruction, and this occurred about forty years later.

city was finally captured, one hundred thousand Jews were taken captive and over one million died. This may have been the worst massacre in one city in all of human history. Israel was destroyed and the Holy City was leveled.

In verses 15–22 Jesus warned the church almost forty years beforehand that Jerusalem was a death-trap and not a city of refuge. The Jewish Christians listened, and fled before Titus closed in with his troops.

In verses 23–28 Jesus told His disciples that the fall of

The Second Coming of Jesus.

Jerusalem was only the beginning of world tumult and not the End itself, but they were to be steadfast in their faith.

In response to the disciples' second question, "What shall be the sign of thy coming?" Jesus promised them that He would come to the earth the second time at the End of the age. So in verses 29–31 He gave them an "unveiling" (or "apocalypse") of the shape of things to come in the traditional manner of Jewish writings about the End. Here Jesus used sombre and restrained poetic symbols like those in Joel 2:10–30, and returned to the Old Testament imagery of the Day of the Lord.

In these ancient biblical pictures, destruction and chaos were always a prelude to re-creation. With this poetic symbolism Jesus pointed to cosmic upheavals that would announce His return to earth in power and glory. For many, His return would be a time of mourning for their part in putting Him to death. Christians, however, will rejoice as the Son delivers the Kingdom to His Father.

At first reading these thirty-one verses seem to be full of doom and gloom, but as I meditate upon them I find at least four clear reasons to be encouraged. First, I feel that Jesus' words assure us that God still controls the world irrespective of the calamities that are foretold. I believe He uses them in His providence to bring into being His rule of righteousness.

Second, we are assured that God is in charge, and as our lives are committed to Him, we move toward a positive goal and a sure future. As we look around us in these closing days of the twentieth century, we see a lot of confusion and lunacy among people and nations. At times, terrorism and strife seem to have the upper hand. But we as Christians can take the longer view and see that God is at work in our world also. He has saved us in the past, He is saving us now, and He most certainly will bring our salvation to full maturity in the future.

Third, in these verses Jesus assures us that evil will finally meet its defeat. On the surface it may look as if Satan rules the world, but when Christ returns it will be to judge and expose evil for the sham and lie that it is. Just as the Pharisees could not defeat Jesus, so evil cannot finally conquer us.

At the same time I believe we Christians need to remember that Satan was defeated at Calvary and on Easter

Sunday morning. We're involved in a mopping-up operation now.

Finally, I believe that in these verses Jesus assures us that at the end of time Christians will be rewarded. We have not only a living hope in this world but in the world to come. Somewhere I read that Albert Schweitzer, the medical missionary to Africa, was in despair one day over his work. He threw himself into a chair in his consulting room and groaned, "What a blockhead I was to come out here to doctor savages like these!" Whereupon his African orderly, Joseph, quietly remarked: "Yes, Doctor, here on earth you are a blockhead, but not in heaven."

The parable of the fig tree.

In verse 32 Jesus refers to the fig tree and how when it began to produce tender buds and then leaves, everyone knew that summer was near. This was a familiar sight in Palestine in Jesus' time. One could easily predict the coming of the seasons by watching the fig trees.

I believe Jesus used this image to illustrate a sign of a coming event, probably to the destruction of Jerusalem. His generation had not yet passed away when the city and the temple finally fell. Salvation and judgment started at His first coming, were present in A.D. 70, are present now, and will continue at His return.

Then in verse 35 He gave us one of the greatest promises of Scripture for both now and in the future when He said, "Heaven and earth shall pass away, but my words shall not pass away." Nothing will last in its present form, not even the heaven and the earth, but His message and work will always endure. Our Jerusalem may fall, our temple may crumble, and we may be scattered as sheep without a shepherd, but the teachings of Jesus are more permanent than the physical world.

The Exhortation to "Be Ready" (24:36–25:46)

The disciples had asked Jesus the question, "Tell us, . . . what shall be the sign of the end of the world?" They naturally wanted to know when the End would take place. Jesus didn't try to avoid their curiosity, and He did tell them of a series of calamities that would happen first. Also, He told them that His gospel would first be preached in all the world. He was certain of His return, but He couldn't tell them the exact day or hour. That time was known only to the Heavenly Father (24:36).

This is a warning for us to avoid speculation. Yes, there

are signs, but since God alone knows the day and the hour, it is more important for us to spend our energies doing God's will—occupying—than trying to be date-setters.

The importance of being ready.

In verses 37–41 Jesus stresses our need to be prepared for His second coming because most people will be surprised by it. As they were in the days of Noah and the Flood, people will be complacently living lives of pleasure and business, giving little thought to God or the future.

There, too, we see especially in verses 40 and 41 that the second coming of Christ will be a time of division and separation—those whose lives have been committed to Him will experience the joy of an endless relationship with God. Those who have rejected Christ will forever be separated from Him. Again, the call is for preparedness.

In another short parable Jesus drives home again the "be prepared" theme (24:42–44). Here He uses the example of a homeowner whose house had been robbed because he had not been watchful. Jesus' advice then, is that we should not become so absorbed in the routine of life that we forget the eternal values. Even as the wise homeowner is prepared for burglars, wise Christians will be watchful and ready for the Day of the Lord.

In these four brief examples Jesus warns us not to be so involved in even the doing of good things that we neglect our personal relationship with God and our witness for Him. Then, too, He urges us to be sensitive to what is going on in the world around us—to be alert, expectant, and prepared for all that the Lord has for us, including an unending relationship with Him.

The parable of the responsible and irresponsible servants.

The next parable is about a servant appointed to look after his master's household while he is away (24:45–51). Jesus used this story to challenge the twelve disciples to be faithful to the work that He had given them to do until He returned. In the story we see the contrast between the "faithful and wise" servant and the "evil" servant.

There is a special word here for every Christian who is involved in any way in the service of the church and its mission in the world. We are urged to be faithful and energetic in our responsibilities; we are to be so connected to the will and purposes of God that our judgments are sound and our planning is good; and we are to be busy and involved in our preparation for Jesus' coming, whenever that is.

This well-known and frequently quoted parable also illustrates the theme of watching or preparing for Christ's second coming (25:1–13). A striking feature of the Jewish wedding ceremony of Jesus' day was the twilight procession which escorted the bridal pair from the home of the bride to the home of the groom. The main characters in this story are ten little wedding-attendant girls waiting for the arrival of the bridegroom. All ten girls are carrying small, shallow lamps so they can be a part of the procession.

The parable of the ten virgins.

But when the bridegroom doesn't arrive on time, the sleepy girls nap. At midnight, however, they are awakened with the news that he is coming. Little oil is left in their lamps because of the long delay, but five of them had the foresight to bring an extra flask of oil for just such an emergency. The other five had been careless and brought no extra oil. In panic they try, unsuccessfully, to borrow some oil from the other five. Their only recourse is to hurry out and buy more.

While they are gone, though, the bridegroom comes, and the five prepared girls lead the bride to the groom's home. The procession takes place without the missing five, and when they finally arrive, it is too late; they are locked out and miss the celebration.

The intent of this story parallels the story of the responsible and irresponsible servants. We are to be watchful and ready. The lamps of our lives are to have the oil of the Holy Spirit.

Jesus told a third parable on the theme of watchful responsibility, but this time He deepened its meaning (25:14–30). The story is about a wealthy man who, leaving on an extended journey, turned some of his money over to three of his servants to manage in his absence. The master gave his most capable servant five talents to manage. To his second most capable man he gave two talents, and to the third he gave one talent.

The parable of the talents.

The five-talent servant handled his money so well that he doubled it; the two-talent servant did the same. But the one-talent servant, fearful that he would lose the money, hid it by burying it in the ground.

When the master returned home, he called in the three servants for an accounting. He praised the first two servants because they had managed his money so well, and he rewarded them with even greater responsibility. But he was very angry with the third servant.

When the third servant gave his weak excuse—fear —for not properly handling the money (25:24), he was condemned, and what he had was taken away from him and given to the servant who had ten talents. He was then thrown out and lost all of the benefits that had been his before.

Jesus makes His point clear in this well-known story. The word "talent" can likely be translated as gifts or opportunities. All of us have received particular gifts and abilities from God. Not all of us have the same gifts, but it is our responsibility to cultivate and use what we have, and as we do this, our gifts will grow and multiply.

But in the story, the third servant is thoroughly condemned. To not use the gifts and abilities God has given us is to lose them—a terrible waste in terms of what could be. The great human tragedy is seen in lost opportunities.

While it is true as Christians that we look expectantly toward whatever God has for us in the future, our responsibility is to use the abilities and gifts He has given us in our daily, nitty-gritty world now. Our role as responsible Christians is to commit our gifts and abilities to God and then use them constructively and creatively in our service for Him.

The final judgment. We have here a vivid picture of the basis on which Jesus will judge the world (25:31–46). It is an awe-inspiring climax to Matthew's fifth Book. It shows the Son of man coming not in humiliation but in glory as we see the church and the world judged by the same standards— Christ's love reflected in our ministry and service to others. Christ's love is the basis of either our acceptance or rejection by a righteous God.

We see Jesus in those verses as the Son of man seated upon the throne of His glory and surrounded by angels. Separated before Him are the people of all time—on His right hand are the righteous ones (sheep) and on His left hand are the unrighteous (goats).

To those on His right He says, "Come . . . inherit the kingdom." He further explains that they are righteous because: "For I was hungry, and ye gave me food; I was thirsty, and ye gave me drink; I was a stranger, and ye took me in; naked and ye clothed me; I was sick and ye visited me; I was in prison, and ye came unto me."

In response to their amazed inquiry as to when they had done all of this for Him, He said, "Inasmuch as ye have done it unto one of the least of these my brethren, ye have done it unto me."

Then turning to the unrighteous ones on His left He says, "Depart from me." In response to their query He indicts them for failing to minister to and meet the needs of people.

From this we understand that our love and devotion to Christ is judged by how much we know of and are moved by the suffering and needs of others. Both what we do and what we don't do determine our acceptance or rejection. And, of course, we are to respond to need out of caring and love, not for possible reward.

Somewhere I read about Ray Villarreal. It seems that every Sunday Villarreal goes to Ciudad Juarez, Mexico, to help the crippled people of that city. He does whatever is necessary including fitting people with artificial limbs and filling prescriptions for corrective shoes.

Evidently he receives some financial help for his work, but he said, "I still pay about ten to twelve thousand dollars, maybe twenty thousand dollars, of my own money every year. But I'll tell you something. I've found that money is round. Spend it in the right direction, and it will come back to you."

In 1981 Ray Villarreal was named "Humanitarian of the Year" by the Italian-American National Hall of Fame. He put feet to the words of Jesus which call for us to so love that we help the sick and those in prison. We have concern for and then act to feed the hungry, provide drink for the thirsty, help clothe those in need, and accept the stranger. To respond in this way to Christ is to one day hear the Good News, "Come, ye blessed of My Father, inherit the kingdom prepared for you from the foundation of the world" (25:34).

Dear Jesus, Thank You for helping me as I learn about You. Help me to "be ready" when You come. Search beyond my external person and see if I am wholly committed to You. Minister to me where I am, Lord.

WHAT THIS SCRIPTURE MEANS TO ME—Matthew 23–25

As I began reading and responding to this lesson, I was reminded of a little boy I knew who joined the childrens' choir in church. After the first rehearsal, his mother asked him how it went.

"Wonderful!" he said. "Before rehearsal they let us play on the playground and afterwards they took us for ice cream."

"But what about the singing?" asked his mother.

"That," he said, "was the only part I didn't like."

Few people find the chapters in our lesson touching on the end of the world their favorite part of Scripture. Yet, as I pondered and began to understand the passages better, I found myself coming into a new and deeper awareness of God's love for us.

Years ago I heard a wonderful story which can provide a steady anchor for us as we read about the "end times."

There was a simple monk working in his garden. A man came to him who was much alarmed, having heard the end of the world was imminent.

"What would you do right now," he asked the monk, "if you knew the end of the world were to come this very afternoon?"

"Finish hoeing my garden," answered the monk, "so that my Lord would find me faithful in the tasks He has given me."

A friend of ours, an accountant, personifies this same spirit. "Some of the reports I am legally required to prepare," he told us, "are never seen, just filed. However, I try to prepare them as if Jesus Himself gave me the assignment."

Conducting his business this way, our friend will always be found faithful, whether the world is ending or continuing.

Jesus' words concerning the importance of our ministering to others harmonize with His parable of the talents. Our service to others is related to the unique gifts we have to give.

A resourceful woman I know noted that many of her friends wore their attractive clothes only a few times before appearing in new ones.

However, many other people of her acquaintance had small wardrobes and tight budgets.

It occurred to her that she had a potential gift as a channel between the two. With a boldness natural to her confident personality, she persuaded her more affluent friends to part with their outfits swiftly. The almost-new clothes then passed through her to others in a steady stream.

This creative use of her talents has been of service to hundreds.

I find it reassuring to remember that our Lord simply asks us to be faithful in our tasks, using our gifts, serving Him in those around us. We can leave everything else concerning the "end times" in His hands.

Sometimes changes occur in our personal lives that, although the world does not end on a cosmic level, we feel as if it's the "end of the world."

When I was nineteen, I had that kind of an experience. At that time, I got married and left family, friends, and home to move, with my husband, two thousand miles away to a small industrial city where I didn't know a soul.

Yet this time of drastic change was lit with a glow of joy because my much loved husband was there with me.

I see the "end times" in a similar way. There may be great changes in our personal lives or on a global scale, but our blessed Lord will be there with us, transforming situations and circumstances with His presence.

LESSON 8
MATTHEW 26–28

Jesus' Death and Resurrection

Father God, Help me to apply this lesson to my life. AMEN.

The passion narrative covers only three days, but all four Gospels devote much of their limited space to a detailed account of the death of Jesus. Why should the Cross of Jesus occupy center stage in His life story? Simply because it is the heart of the gospel and was the core of the church's teaching from the beginning. Jesus did much for us in His life, but He did even more for us through His death and resurrection.

Chapter 26 of Matthew covers the events of Wednesday and Thursday after Jesus had finished His teaching on the Mount of Olives. Chapter 27 begins with Jesus' trial before the high priest Caiaphas on Friday morning and ends with His burial Friday evening. Chapter 28 begins with Easter Sunday morning before dawn and concludes some days later back in Galilee where Jesus commissioned His disciples to be apostles to the whole world.

The Preparation for the Death of Jesus (26:1–75)

The great passion and resurrection section is the climax of Matthew's Gospel. The Jewish leaders had decided to reject Jesus as their Messiah. The assassination of Jesus was the inevitable consequence of their choice. Jesus had already anticipated and accepted their cruel rejection of Him.

In this chapter there are certain highlights Matthew

wants us to focus on. He says that God's way of accomplishing our salvation is mysterious indeed. He can use any means in His providential purpose: the scheming of evil men, the sentimental gift of a devout lady, a disaffected disciple who tries to play God, the ancient religious ceremonies of Israel, lying witnesses, friends who panic under stress, and the stomach-wrenching horror and humiliation of crucifixion. Most mysterious of all, Jesus, who did not desire death, accepted God's will which did include death.

In the Gospel of Matthew Jesus talked about His death at least twelve times before it happened. In chapter 26:1–2 He made His fourth deliberate prediction to the disciples that He would be killed. This time He added that it would be two days away, during the Passover, and that He would be crucified at the hands of the Romans. Jesus associated His death with the sacrifice of the Passover lamb.

The official religious and political body, the Sanhedrin, was plotting Jesus' death at the palace of Caiaphas the high priest, but the timing was a problem for them (26:3–5). They feared a premature uprising that would embroil the whole nation with Rome and terminate their own privileged position of religious leadership.

Jewish leaders plot Jesus' death.

The leaders agreed that Jesus should be killed quietly, but not during Passover. Above all else, it was important to avoid any kind of public disturbance, otherwise a revolution could erupt and the whole delicate political-religious balance would be upset.

In contrast to the murder being plotted in Jerusalem Matthew now gives us the story of a woman coming to Jesus at Bethany to anoint Him with a special ointment (26:6–13). John's Gospel (12:3) says that the woman was Mary, the sister of Martha and Lazarus.

Jesus anointed in Simon's home.

During ther meal at Simon's house Mary poured a vial of very expensive perfume or ointment on the head of Jesus. It was probably spikenard from far-off India (Mk: 14:3) and may have been her greatest treasure (the equivalent of a laborer's year's wages).

Her generous act touched the heart of Jesus, and in the days to come it made a deep impression on the early church. Mary, by her love, provided Jesus with the last encouragement for the work He had to do, and this is why she will always be remembered. But the disciples, shackled by their materialism, missed the spiritual meaning of Mary's act.

In fact the disciples became indignant at what they considered a waste of money. They said "the ointment might have been sold for much, and given to the poor." But Jesus defended her extravagant love and commended her beautiful spirit.

It is easy for us to become so overly involved with life's routine that our values become discolored. Or we miss the "better" because we can only see the "good." An artist and a timber merchant stood together watching a beautiful sunset throw its golden light over a green forest of trees. The artist said, "It is glorious, isn't it?" The merchant replied, "Yes, that is fresh timber, and I think that allowing for cutting and transportation it should work out to about a dollar a foot."

The treachery of Judas.

In contrast to Mary's generosity is the treachery of Judas (26:14–16). Judas betrayed Jesus for the equivalent of about $25. Naturally we don't know Judas' motive, but there is every reason to believe that he had anticipated all along that Jesus was to be a nationalistic Messiah who would free the Jews from Roman occupation and restore glory to Israel. If that was the case, it is possible he finally came to see that Jesus was going to be a Suffering Servant Messiah instead, and out of anger and disillusionment Judas plotted the betrayal. On the other hand, he may still have seen Jesus as a political Messiah. He may have thought confronting Jesus would force Him to discard His humble disguise and openly revolt against their oppressive Roman conquerors. In taking this course Judas fell into the trap that has plagued the Christian church ever since—attempting to reshape Jesus to fit our own purposes.

Celebrating the Passover.

We don't know about Jesus' activities on Wednesday of Holy Week, but it may have been a day of rest and retreat for Him in preparation for the Passover meal on Thursday. However, in 26:17–19 we read of the discussion between the disciples and Jesus about arrangements for celebrating the Jewish exodus from Egypt under Moses. Custom dictated that the meal be eaten in Jerusalem where space was scarce because of the thousands of pilgrims who had arrived to celebrate the Passover. Apparently, though, Jesus had already arranged for a secret meeting place and told the disciples to find a certain man in the city and give him the message that He and His disciples would eat the Passover meal at his house.

The arrangements were completed and on Thursday evening Jesus and His disciples ate the Passover evening meal (26:20–25).

During the meal Jesus announced the shattering prediction that one of the twelve disciples would betray Him. In consternation and sorrow each one asked, "Lord, is it I?" Their question carries the implication, "It surely could not be I, could it?"

None of the eleven suspected Judas, and they even seemed a little uncertain of their own loyalty in the coming crisis. If Judas had been the obvious monster that we tend to picture Him today the disciples surely would have doubted him. Leonardo da Vinci was probably wrong in the way he portrayed Judas in his famous painting of the Lord's Supper. For a whole year, da Vinci said, he visited the lowest quarters of Milan until he finally found a villain with a face evil enough to serve as a model for his picture of Judas. Even then, he said, he added to it all the worst in other faces he had seen.

It was only a brief two or three hours now before the storm would break over Jesus in devastating fury, but here in the quiet upper room He initiated the great Christian meal of all ages (26:26–30). Here we are on sacred and mysterious ground, for into the ordered solemnity of the Passover meal Jesus inserted words (26:28–29) that turned the event into the Lord's Supper.

When my children were small and we observed the Lord's Supper in a worship service, they asked, "What are you doing that for?" To answer them and to help satisfy myself, I explained that participating in the Lord's Supper reminds me of the depth of Jesus' love for me. It is also a time when I pledge my loyalty to Christ anew. Then, too, during those solemn moments I feel uniquely bound in fellowship with my Christian brothers and sisters, both nearby and around the world. Finally, I am reminded that Christ has promised to come again (26:29).

Jesus' sacred words about His "body" and "blood" speak of a *new* covenant between God and people everywhere. His symbolic words pointed to His death on the cross as an atonement for sin. By His death Jesus brought the New

An ancient olive tree in the Garden of Gethsemane. This particular tree is said to be over 2,000 years old and may have witnessed the agony and arrest of Jesus.

Israel (the church) into being, and the Last Supper was a foretaste of the Messianic Banquet at the end of time. The old Passover recalled God's deliverance from death; the new Passover freed people from their old sins to new life in Christ. By shedding His blood, Jesus became the new Passover sacrifice.

After they had sung a hymn at the conclusion of the meal, Jesus and the disciples left the secret upper room and walked over to the Mount of Olives where He told them they would become discouraged and leave Him that night (26:30–35). He was speaking, of course, of His arrest and execution, but He also told them He would be raised from the dead and would then meet with them in Galilee.

Cocksure Peter said that he would never desert Him, but Jesus told him that before that night was over he would deny Him three times. Jesus knew Peter better than Peter knew himself. And He knows us better than we know ourselves. Like Peter, we sometimes think we know better than Jesus how we will act in a crisis. So often we trust in our own knowledge and wisdom when we should be turning to God for help. And again like Peter, we too easily trust our own determination and willpower to sustain us during difficulties.

On the slope of the two-mile-long Mount of Olives nestled a garden called Gethsemane. Jesus led His disciples there to wrestle in prayer over the test that was now only a short time away (26:36–46). Like His baptismal experience over three years before, Jesus was surrounded by temptation. Would He save Himself or would He save others? He could have escaped north to Galilee and avoided Judas or have just passively given up, or He could have accepted His fate in righteous indignation as John the Baptist had done. Instead, He turned to the Heavenly Father in prayer, and chose the "inner circle" of Peter, James, and John to share His anguish.

After asking Peter, James, and John to stand vigil with Him, Jesus went on alone to pray, "O my Father, if it be possible, let this cup pass from me..." Returning to where He had left the three disciples, He found them sleeping. Again He asked them to watch and pray with Him, and Jesus prayed once more, "O my Father, if this cup may not pass away from me, except I drink it, thy will be done."

A second time Jesus found His three friends sound asleep, and a third time Jesus prayed "saying the same words." Then we see him waking Peter, James, and John again. Jesus had been through the severest test of His ministry, but He had come out of this prayer experience with

Jesus warns the disciples.

Jesus prays in Gethsemane.

confidence and bravery that God's will would be done.

There is no way we can even begin to understand the physical and spiritual agony Jesus experienced in the garden that night. Was it because He'd been rejected by His countrymen? Was it because He knew His disciples would soon desert Him? Was His heaviest burden knowing that shortly the load of our sin would rest on His shoulders, and that He would be completely alone?

We don't know. But again we see in Jesus that through prayer the resources can be ours to handle any and all forms of rejection and suffering. We see, too, that God will give us the fortitude and the victory to remain steady in our faith irrespective of outer circumstances.

On the night of February 3, 1943, the U.S.S. *Dorchester* was torpedoed by an enemy submarine in the North Atlantic and sank. Among the many who died were four chaplains. One of the four was Clark Poling, son of a clergyman, who, just before sailing, asked his father, "Just pray that I shall do my duty . . . that I shall be adequate."

When the crippled ship was sinking, it became obvious that there weren't enough life jackets to go around, so Poling and his three fellow chaplains took theirs off and gave them to four men who didn't have any. Then the four chaplains joined hands in prayer as the ship slipped beneath the surface. Poling's prayer was answered—he was adequate, even as was his Lord when He left His place of prayer in the garden.

The arrest and trial of Jesus.

Judas arrived at the garden of Gethsemane with an armed crowd of temple police to arrest Jesus (26:47–56). Since the arresting officers didn't know Him, Judas identified Him by kissing Him. Even now Jesus greeted Judas by calling him "Friend." By doing this, it is possible He was signaling Judas that there was still time to change his mind. The patience of our Lord goes way beyond the bounds of our imagination!

But whatever Judas' motives were, he had no intention of changing his plans. He was too committed to the other side, and he must have watched the arrest of Jesus with some satisfaction.

Jesus didn't intend to resist arrest, but as the men moved in on Him one of the disciples (the Gospel of John says it was Simon Peter) whipped out his sword and attacked the mob. Peter had anticipated violence and was ready to be violent in return. But Jesus would not let Peter use his sword for Him, and the confused disciples ran away into the night leaving Jesus alone with His captors. The die was cast; Jesus would not resort to the available power (26:53) in self-interest. He would establish His Kingdom with a cross, not a sword. Jesus knew that "all they that take the sword shall perish with the sword." Violence only breeds violence.

Next we see Jesus in the palace of the high priest before the Sanhedrin sometime after midnight (26:57–68) and again at dawn (27:1). We are also told that while Peter ran from the garden with the other disciples at the time of Jesus' arrest, he came back and followed the arresting mob to the high priest's courtyard, and there "sat with the guards, to see the end."

The Sanhedrin was in session waiting for Jesus when He was brought in. The council had already decided that Jesus had to die, but to make it legal they had to come up very quickly with a good charge in order to sentence Him to death.

After grueling hours of conflicting testimony, two witnesses agreed that Jesus had claimed to be able to destroy Jerusalem's temple and rebuild it in three day's time. This, of course, was a complete distortion of His words, but they had what they wanted, since to speak against the temple was considered blasphemy. Jesus refused to defend Himself against the perjured testimony because He knew the Sanhedrin was already determined to execute Him. The verdict had been settled before the trial had begun.

A charge of blasphemy would have been ignored by Pilate so they needed to manufacture a political charge. Caiaphas then asked Jesus if He were the Christ (Messiah), hoping He would say "Yes," so he could charge Him with being a revolutionary and a threat to Rome. Jesus said, "Yes," and Caiaphas had what he wanted. Jesus could be charged with blasphemy before the Jews and with being a political revolutionary before Pilate, the Roman ruler. Only the political crime of claiming to be the Jewish Messiah (King of the Jews and therefore an enemy of the Roman Emperor) would compel Pilate to pass the death sentence on Friday morning. The Sanhedrin did its part in the drama by giving Jesus the death penalty.

Let's pause now in our story for a closer look at Caiaphas, the prime participant in the murder of Jesus. For Matthew he is the essence of everything that had gone wrong in Judaism. Matthew uses his example as a summary of everything that a good Christian leader should work to avoid, while Jesus under stress is a picture of everything we should be. This contrast has four things to say to us.

First, Jesus found strength and courage in His submission to God's will, even though His "cup" meant the cross. Our true strength, whether we are church leaders or not, grows out of saying "thy will be done."

Second, Jesus was candid in His answers to the Sanhedrin. He admitted that He was the Messiah, but He explained that He was no political threat to the Sanhedrin or the Romans. Caiaphas, on the other hand, was a shrewd, clever actor, with a gift for the theatrical gesture. He used these skills to execute Jesus rather than discover the truth. As Christians we must "let honesty be our only policy." A great fire swept through a western city over half a century ago. After the flames died down, all the chimneys built by one particular firm in that city were standing while those built by other firms had been destroyed. The standing chimneys bore an inscription saying, "This chimney was built by _____ and Company who are still doing honest work for their customers." Jesus was honest—Caiaphas was not.

In the third place, Jesus depended upon the protective care of God. He requested no special favors, no haven of security, and no financial reward for His services. Caiaphas was just the opposite—he was the champion of the fallacious entrenched system that put him in office—any proposed change to his own special interests was looked upon as traitorous heresy. He was the worst distortion of a religious leader—his office had become a cloak for his own selfish ambitions. He was willing to crucify anyone to retain his power. No Christian among us can have God's blessings if we don't rid ourselves of the cloak of Caiaphas.

And fourth, Jesus put His trust in God's love to win and change our hearts. He knew that our self-respect must remain intact if we are to be won to His cause. We cannot be threatened or brutalized into the Kingdom of God. But Caiaphas was an unscrupulous scoundrel to whom the truth meant nothing. Love and compassion were his enemies, and power politics was all he knew about moving people.

The scene shifts to the courtyard of the high priest's palace, and we find Peter there with the servants (26:69–75). During the course of the evening three different people had tried to associate him with Jesus. At first Peter denied it, then he swore an oath that he did not know Jesus, and finally with great intensity and another oath he insisted again that he did not know Jesus. At that moment Peter heard the cock crow and he remembered Jesus' prediction. Overcome by his betrayal, he "went out and wept bitterly."

Peter himself must have told the story to the church in later days. To confess his denial must have taken extraordinary courage. Peter probably used his own story to illustrate the compassionate caring and complete forgiveness of Jesus. He made no effort to excuse his failure.

William Barclay, the Scottish commentator on the New Testament, tells about an evangelist in his country named Brownlow North. He had lived a wild life as a youth, and he was reminded of it one Sunday morning in Aberdeen. Before he entered the pulpit to preach, a letter was handed to him, and the writer threatened to reveal a shameful incident in North's past before he became a Christian. North took the letter into the pulpit with him, read it to the congregation, and told them he was guilty. Then he told them how Christ had forgiven him and how he was now a new person. He used his sin to draw others to Christ just as Peter did after his betrayal of Jesus.

Peter denies Jesus.

Matthew tells us that early on Friday morning the Sanhedrin met and ratified its decision of Thursday night (27:1–2). Criminal cases had to be handled and concluded in the daytime according to Jewish law. Jesus was then handed over to Pilate, the representative of civil power. Since the Sanhedrin lacked the power to put Jesus to death it had to rely on Rome for the execution.

When Judas realized that Jesus had actually been condemned, he repented of his betrayal and returned the thirty pieces of silver to the elders and chief priests (27:3–20). But they wouldn't reconsider their action against Jesus, and in

The Crucifixion of Jesus (27:1–66)

The infamy of Pilate and Judas.

despair, Judas threw down the money in the temple and committed suicide.

What a tragic end for a man with the potential for greatness. It isn't likely that he had originally intended to betray Jesus. But selfish gain and a hunger for power so distorted his thinking that he has become the epitome of evil ever since.

While at first we might not think so, the story of Judas leaves us with some important lessons. First, I believe, Judas tried to "play God" in an effort to manipulate Jesus' actions. By contrast, as we have looked closely at the life of Jesus in these lessons, we have seen that Jesus never used people. There was nothing manipulative about His teaching.

We also see in Judas that there is no human remedy for a guilty conscience. Only through our repentance and prayer can God set our minds and consciences at rest. It is God who forgives our sin. The double tragedy of Judas is that he could have repented before God even as Peter had. As with Peter, he would have been forgiven.

We learn through this story also about the callousness of the priests and elders of Israel, and how our consciences can learn to tolerate wickedness and sin if we are not careful. They observed the proprieties of religion but had nothing of its spirit. In the process, they substituted the form of religion for actual faith.

Early Friday morning Jesus stood before Pilate accused of treason against Rome (27:11–14). Pilate's question, "Are you the King of the Jews?" implied a charge of high treason. When Jesus, with reserve and courtesy, answered "Yes," He infuriated the Jews and they hurled their accusations at Him.

But as Pilate observed the scene, he didn't believe the charge of rebellion against the state. He was astute enough to see that Jesus was not dangerous, and he was made uncomfortable by Jesus' refusal to noisily defend Himself.

Then Pilate tried to release Jesus under the amnesty of the feast (27:15–23). At Passover a custom of the governors was to release a prisoner for the people, and Pilate tried to use this practice to gain Jesus' freedom. In order to preserve justice he proposed a trade. He placed beside Jesus a rebel named Barabbas who had taken up arms against Rome and asked the Jews to choose which prisoner he should release to them. He tried to force them to ask for Jesus, but he failed. His attempt to free Jesus was finally frustrated by the veiled threat of the Jewish leaders who cast doubt on his loyalty to Caesar (John 19:12).

During the trial a message came from Pilate's wife which warned her husband to "have nothing to do with" the righteous Jesus. She had dreamed about Jesus and the dream had disturbed her greatly.

Meanwhile, the elders and the chief priests incited the crowd against Jesus. The mob shouted for the release of Barabbas and the death of Jesus. This put Pilate in a tough situation because he knew that if he released Jesus a serious riot might get started (27:24–26). He had to keep peace in Jerusalem to retain his position, and for that he needed the help of the elders and chief priests. But to sentence the innocent Jesus to death would be a betrayal of Roman justice. So he finally "washed his hands" of the whole affair.

While preparations were being made for the crucifixion, the Roman soldiers took Jesus into their quarters and began to ridicule Him (27:27–31). They dressed Him in a royal robe and put a crown of thorns on His head and then knelt before Him in contempt. With barracks room humor they spat in His face and hit Him. Finally, tiring of the cruel game, they put Jesus' own clothes back on Him and led Him to His execution.

Jesus is crucified.

Jesus started the march toward death with open wounds from which His blood flowed. Because He was weak He stumbled under the load of the crossbar on the way to Golgotha (27:32–44), and Simon of Cyrene was pulled out of the crowd to carry the cross for Him.

Jesus was crucified at nine o'clock Friday morning, and died six hours later at three o'clock in the afternoon. As a means of execution crucifixion was a terrible ordeal, but Matthew relates the event with a minimum of words. Matthew does not stress, as we so often do, Jesus' physical pain. Instead he emphasizes the spiritual strain—Christ died, yes, but He died for *our sins.* Christ's death changed our relationship to God, for God was in Christ "reconciling the world to Himself."

With macabre indifference the soldiers divided His garments by lot (gambling), and then stood by to make sure there weren't any attempts to interfere with the execution.

Raised only a foot or two above the bystanders Jesus could easily hear and be heard. With tongue-in-cheek some in the crowd challenged Him to get down from the cross and save Himself. Even the two who suffered with Him joined in the scoffing. The whole world seemed to have rejected the Son of God. It was a dismal hour.

The death of Jesus was such a cruel miscarriage of justice that we usually think of the men who did it as monsters. But they were just ordinary people going about the business of living in their society even as we are today in ours. Let's reflect on them for a moment. Who really was responsible for Jesus' death?

The soldiers who actually put Jesus to death were only doing their duty. A soldier is paid to do stern, cruel things when he is commanded to, and crucifixion was part of their business as professionals. They simply did their work as they were told.

Organized business of that day was also responsible. The money changers in the temple (the Sadducees and their clerks) were pleased with their big profits, and when Jesus touched this sensitive nerve, they moved to protect their income. One American economist has said that the major iniquities of our time are connected with money-making since many people feel a business has a right to be profitable, even if it must abandon its integrity.

The official established religion was involved in Jesus' death. The scribes and Pharisees believed in God and His Law, and they were respected leaders in their community. But when Jesus threatened their interpretation of religion they had to get rid of the blasphemer.

Political expediency put Jesus to death. Caiaphas and Pilate, both expert politicians, were playing it safe as politicians frequently do. Both were trying to prevent a public uproar, and we recognize in their motives the common practices of popular politics today. So often expediency determines our thinking and actions.

We see ourselves in so much of this. When I'm tempted to be judgmental of Jesus' executioners, I find myself praying instead, God forgive us for what we are still doing to Him today.

From noon until 3:00 P.M. on that Friday an unusual phenomenon of darkness covered the countryside (27:45–50). Then about three o'clock Jesus cried out with the words of Psalm 22:1, "My God, my God, why hast thou forsaken me?" Jesus, like the Psalm writer, must have felt desperately alone in His suffering, yet the Psalm ends in trium-

The Church of the Holy Sepulchre in Jerusalem. Here can be seen the roof top and domes of the church which covers the traditional site of the crucifixion and burial of Jesus.

phant faith. Jesus' statement of loneliness and desperation is too profound for us to fathom. The full pain to the Godhead in bearing our sin can never be known to us. Then Matthew tells us that after another loud cry Jesus was dead; He had given His life.

The executioners didn't take Jesus' life—He voluntarily gave it up. And here is the central paradox of Matthew's Gospel and the lesson above all others that he wants us to learn: the cross of Jesus looked like a crushing defeat of righteousness, and yet it was one of the greatest victories that righteousness ever won. Jesus knew that to fail as He did was the only way to succeed. For He said, "He who finds his life will lose it, and he who loses his life for my sake will find it."

161

Matthew stressed three unusual events that attended His death: the curtain of the temple was torn in two from top to bottom, symbolizing that now all people have ready access to God; the earth quaked, symbolizing the cosmic nature of His death; and some of the dead saints were raised from their graves, symbolizing the immortality that awaits all Christians (27:51–56). Further, the Roman centurian was convinced of Jesus' integrity when he confessed, "Truly this was the Son of God."

Jesus in the tomb.

Jesus was dead, and according to Deuteronomy 21:23 His body had to be removed from the cross before nightfall. Joseph of Arimathea, a wealthy member of the Sanhedrin and a secret disciple of Jesus, immediately asked Pilate for the body so it could be buried in his new family tomb (27:57–61). Joseph showed a unique devotion to Jesus since criminals were not supposed to be buried in family tombs—he risked offending the Jews by his action.

Pilate granted Joseph's request, and Jesus' body was buried before the Sabbath (Saturday) began at sunset on Friday night. At least two of Jesus' female followers from Galilee, Mary Magdalene and the other Mary, watched His burial, as they had also watched His crucifixion.

On the next day (the Sabbath, or Saturday) the Pharisees and chief priests went to Pilate and told him that Jesus had promised to rise from the dead three days after His death (27:62–66). They feared that His disciples would steal His body and perpetrate the fraud that He had risen. They asked Pilate to guard the tomb for three days, since in Jewish thinking a person's spirit left the body after that time. Pilate agreed and sent a group of soldiers to seal the tomb and guard it.

The Resurrection of Jesus (28:1–20)

As dawn was breaking on Sunday morning Mary Magdalene and Mary the mother of James and Joseph came to the tomb, eager to perform the proper burial rights on the body of Jesus which they could not do on the Sabbath (28:1–8).

An empty tomb.

Matthew describes the scene, "...there was a great earthquake: for the angel of the Lord descended from heaven, and came and rolled back the stone from the door, and sat upon it. His countenance was like lightning, and his raiment white as snow". . . and the guards "became as dead men." Matthew pictures these two events for his

Jewish readers in the familiar terms of Old Testament miracles, assuring them that these stupendous events came from the God of Israel.

The women were almost as shocked as the awe-stricken guards, but the angel reassured them with a comforting message. He told them that Jesus was raised from the dead as He had predicted, and they could verify this by looking at the empty tomb. Then the angel sent them on a mission to find the disciples, tell them Jesus was resurrected and that He would meet them in Galilee. From the other Gospels we learn that Jesus appeared to His disciples while they were still in Jerusalem, but for Matthew the most important appearance was the one in Galilee. With both fear and great joy the two women ran to tell the news.

No book ever written ends with such triumph as does Matthew's Gospel. The angel spoke with hope and assurance—both the cross and the tomb were now empty because Christ was risen from the dead.

Matthew tells us that as the two women ran, Jesus Himself met them (28:8–10). It was the same Jesus that had been buried on Friday, and He greeted them with the familiar and simple "Hail" (or "rejoice"). They grasped His body in adoration, the physical contact giving them a double assurance that it was actually Jesus and not a ghost. He was still the Jesus they knew, but now they respected Him as their risen Lord who deserved the worship that belonged to God.

What did this personal encounter mean to the two women, and what can it mean to us? First, they were convinced that the one who had been in the tomb was the same person who came out three days later. He wasn't a ghost. In being convinced of this amazing truth their confidence in God was restored. All the trust they had put in God seemed to be one huge mistake when Jesus was killed, but now their faith in God's love and power must have come surging back as they clasped His pierced feet. The Father had not deserted Him on the cross, but had used His death to bring salvation to all people. And we, too, take heart, knowing that even during our most miserable days, God is still with us.

Also we see in this glorious event the guarantee of our own immortality. As long as Jesus was in the tomb, we would have every right to fear death. But if Christ is risen, then we know that we too shall live beyond the grave. For

Mary Magdalene and the other Mary and for us, life and immortality are assured after a personal encounter with the risen Lord.

As usual, Matthew is great on details, for now he digresses long enough to tell the plight of the Roman guards (28:11–15). The tomb was empty, and they knew they were responsible. As good soldiers, they walked to Jerusalem and told the chief priests about the supernatural events which they saw.

The religious authorities responded by bribing the guards to keep quiet—to say that the disciples had stolen the body while they slept. The soldiers accepted the hush money and the assurance of the authorities that they wouldn't be punished if Pilate heard the story.

Jesus and the disciples in Galilee.

The eleven disciples and possibly many other followers of Jesus traveled north to Galilee as Jesus had instructed them (28:16–20). They met Him at a designated mountain, possibly the same one where He had commissioned them as apostles.

When some of the disciples saw Jesus, the fact of His presence was almost too good to believe. Physical sight helps immensely, but the eyes of faith are indispensable to understand the real significance of the risen Christ.

A great claim, a great commission, and a great promise.

Matthew ends his Gospel with a great claim (28:18), a great commission (28:19), and a great promise (28:20).

By His victory over death Jesus claimed that He was invested with the power and authority of God Himself (28:18). He said, "All power is given unto me in heaven and in earth." In His thirty-three years Jesus had accepted all the limitations of being human. But in His resurrected body He reasserted all the prerogatives that had belonged to Him as the pre-existent eternal Son of the Father.

This claim means that Jesus was clearly the Son of God. On Friday morning He had been rejected by His people and put to death. On Sunday morning He was vindicated by God the Father and raised from the dead.

As the powerful Son of God He is able, as He promised, to give us power to meet all the demands of life. Even as He conquered death and the grave, we know that our own Good Fridays of defeat and despair are but first steps to an Easter of triumph.

Next we hear Jesus give the great commission (28:19).

Since all power belonged to Him, He had the authority to require their obedience as He said to them and us, "Go ye therefore, and teach all nations, baptizing them in the name of the Father, and of the Son, and of the Holy Ghost."

According to this command, we are on a worldwide venture. We are to represent Him everywhere. Matthew's Gospel has been moving toward this commission since the Jewish genealogy in Chapter 1. The universal covenant with Abraham was fulfilled in the risen Christ and His Gospel. Jesus gave the commission in "Galilee of the gentiles" with its missionary associations. For the most part Jesus had restricted His ministry to Israel, but the disciples were to launch a world mission of bringing everyone under the teaching and rule of Jesus.

He expects the same from us that He expected of the eleven apostles—to share what we have received. Jesus Himself is the content of our message—He *is* the Gospel.

A third part of the commission refers to baptism. By baptizing in the Father's name the new disciple is assured that God is *above* him or her as creator, possessor, and protector. By baptizing in the Son's name the new disciple has confidence that God is *for* him or her through His incarnation, crucifixion, and redemption. And baptism in the name of the Holy Spirit assures the new disciple that God is now *in* him or her, and is actively at work.

In verse 20 Jesus gives us the great promise that we will never be alone. The never-failing Christ will be with us as friend and Savior. Whenever we make the venture as disciples, Christ is by our side. Emmanuel, "God with us," will be with us until the end of time.

Matthew began his Gospel with Christ and he ends it the same way. Through us the world is called to acknowledge and obey Christ. The world will be saved only in Christ. And Christ is what the Gospel of Matthew is all about.

Dear Lord, I can boast in knowing about You! I am deeply and eternally grateful to You for the magnificent sacrifice You made for my sins. Mary had things in perspective when she spent a year's salary in anointing You for Your burial. Give me that kind of vision of Yourself, Lord.

WHAT THIS SCRIPTURE MEANS TO ME—Matthew 26–28

This lesson has become one of the most special to me. The circumstances under which I came to the end of it harmonized with the Scripture in an unforgettable way.

I began this particular reading of the last chapters in Matthew on a spring morning in the garden of some friends.

As I moved into the familiar chapters, the story of the woman in Simon's house at Bethany who anointed the Lord with precious ointment, caught my attention. Touched by the generous outpouring of her love, I was reminded of my mother-in-law.

I remembered a time when my husband, Bill, and I were visiting her with our three children. One of the children admired a lovely and valuable painting she had of the Texas hill country.

My mother-in-law carefully lifted it off the wall. "It's yours," she said, handing it to our daughter.

Aware that Bill's mother was not in a financial position to replace it easily, I protested.

"Oh, Honey," she responded, "I only wish I had ten more to give her."

A visiting speaker at our church once said, "To love is to give of one's best to the one loved." Jesus makes it clear through His life and teaching that love and giving are inseparable.

And then, as I continued my reflection on the last three chapters in Matthew, I came to Jesus' prayer in Gethsemane, "Thy will be done." Many years ago, perplexed by this passage, I had taken it to Bill.

"Why," I asked, "would God's will be for His Son to go to the cross?"

"God's will," Bill answered gently, "was that Jesus remain His faithful Son. But, in so doing, Jesus inevitably came into conflict with the evil in men. Men, by their sin, necessitated His crucifixion, not God."

Many experience their own personal Gethsemanes. A friend of ours became aware of dishonest practices in the company he worked for. Since the company wouldn't change, he left his job.

His Gethsemane involved deciding to do the right thing, despite the cost to himself. He had, however, a "Third Day" experience, for the work he subsequently found turned out to be the most fulfilling of his career.

As I came to the closing words in Matthew's Gospel, I was still in our friends' garden.

The brightness of that morning was dazzling. Washed fresh by a night thunderstorm, the leaves and grass sparkled with raindrops. Birds dipped and soared, trailing glad songs behind them. New blooming roses tumbled over the fence. The fragrance and glorious colors of spring spoke of joy and celebration.

In this setting I read again Matthew's vivid account of the resurrection. Jesus' victory over death and evil, together with the glory of the spring morning in which I read, were in exquisite harmony. The combined message of New Life was intense and breathtaking.

Years ago I heard Gert Behanna, the converted alcoholic and popular Christian witness of a generation ago, tell a story which gathers together in a few words what is, to me, a dominant theme in our lesson.

Coming late to faith, Gert lamented to her son that she had so few years left to follow Christ.

"It's all right, Mom," he answered. "This trip is forever."

SPECIFIC MIRACLES OF JESUS IN MATTHEW

1. Jesus heals a leper after delivering the Sermon on the Mount — 8:1–4
2. Jesus heals the paralyzed servant of a centurian in Capernaum — 8:5–13
3. Jesus heals the fever of Peter's mother-in-law — 8:14–15
4. Jesus calms the storm on the Sea of Galilee — 8:23–27
5. Jesus heals two demon-possessed men of Gadara — 8:28–34
6. The paralyzed man healed at Capernaum — 9:1–8
7. Jesus restores life to an official's (Jairus) daughter in Capernaum — 9:18–19; 23–26
8. Jesus heals a woman with a hemorrhage in Capernaum — 9:20–22
9. Jesus restores sight to two blind men in Capernaum — 9:27–31
10. A devil cast out of a dumb man in Capernaum — 9:32–34
11. Jesus heals the man with a withered hand — 12:9–14
12. The feeding of the 5,000 with five loaves and two fish — 14:13–21
13. Jesus walks on the water (Sea of Galilee) — 14:22–33
14. Jesus heals the daughter of a Canaanite woman in the region of Tyre and Sidon — 15:21–28
15. The feeding of 4,000 with seven loaves and a few fish — 15:32–38
16. Jesus heals a lunatic boy — 17:14–21
17. Jesus provides money from a fish's mouth to pay the Capernaum tax collector — 17:24–27
18. Jesus restores sight to two blind men on the Jericho road — 20:29–34
19. At Jesus' command the barren fig tree dies — 21:18–22

THE PARABLES OF JESUS IN MATTHEW

1. Two builders—one built a house on sand; the other built on solid rock — 7:24–27
2. The Sower — 13:4–9; 18–23
3. The Wheat and the Tares (darnel) — 13:24–30; 36–43
4. The Mustard Seed — 13:31–32
5. The Leaven (yeast) — 13:33
6. Treasure Hidden in a Field — 13:44
7. The Pearl of Great Value — 13:45
8. The Net (dragnet) — 13:47–50
9. The Lost Sheep — 18:12–13
10. The Unmerciful (unforgiving) Servant — 18:23–35
11. Laborers (workers) in the Vineyard — 20:1–16
12. A Man and His Two Sons — 21:28–32
13. The Landowner and His Wicked Husbandmen — 21:33–44
14. Marriage of a King's Son and the Wedding Feast — 22:1–14
15. The Fig Tree Putting Out Leaves — 24:32
16. The Wise and Foolish Virgins — 25:1–13
17. A Man, His Servants, and the Talents — 25:14–30

A HARMONY OF THE GOSPELS

	MATTHEW	MARK	LUKE	JOHN
The genealogy of Jesus	1:1–17		3:23–38	
The birth of John the Baptist			1:5–25; 57–80	
The birth of Jesus	1:5–25; 2:1		2:1–20	
The wise men find Jesus	2:1–12			
The flight to Egypt	2:13–23			
The boy Jesus at the temple			2:41–50	
John the Baptist preaches and baptizes	3:1–12	1:1–8	3:1–20	
Jesus' baptism	3:13–17	1:9–11	3:21–22	
Jesus' temptation	4:1–11	1:12–13	4:1–13	
Jesus' first miracle at Cana				2:1–11
Jesus and Nicodemus				3:1–21
Jesus and the Samaritan woman				4:5–42
Jesus heals the nobleman's son				4:46–54
Jesus selects four disciples	4:18–22	1:16–20	5:1–11	
Demon-possessed man healed		1:23–28	4:31–37	
Jesus gives the Sermon on the Mount	5:1—7:29		6:20–49	
The parable of the two builders	7:24–27		6:47–49	
Jesus heals a leper	8:1–4	1:40–45	5:12–14	
The centurion's servant healed	8:5–13		7:1–10	
Peter's mother-in-law healed	8:14–15	1:29–31	4:38–39	
Life restored to the widow's son			7:11–17	
Jesus calms the storm	8:23–27	4:36–41	8:22–25	
Demon-possessed men healed	8:28–34	5:1–21	8:26–40	
Paralyzed man healed	9:1–8	2:3–12	5:18–26	
Life restored to Jairus' daughter	9:18–19, 23–26	5:22–24, 35–43	8:41–42, 49–56	
Woman healed of hemorrhage	9:20–22	5:25–34	8:43–48	
Blind man healed (Capernaum)	9:27–31			
Devil cast out of dumb man	9:32–34			

	Matthew	Mark	Luke	John
The disciples sent on tour	10:1—11:1	6:7-13	9:1-6	
Man with withered hand healed	12:9-14	3:1-5	6:6-11	
The parable of the sower	13:4–9, 18–23	4:1-20	8:14-15	
The parable of the tares	13:24-30			
The parable of the mustard seed	13:31-32	4:30-32	13:20-21	
The parable of the leaven	13:33-34			
The parable of hidden treasure	13:44			
The parable of the pearl	13:45			
The parable of the net	13:47-50			
John the Baptist killed	14:1-12	6:14-29	9:7-9	
The feeding of the 5,000	14:13-21	6:33-44	9:11-17	6:1-14
Jesus walks on the sea	14:22-33	6:45-52		6:15-21
Canaanite woman's daughter healed	15:21-28	7:24-30		
The feeding of the 4,000	15:32-38	8:1-9		
Blind man at Bethsaida healed		8:22-26		
Peter's great confession	16:13-26	8:27-37	9:18-25	
The transfiguration of Jesus	16:27—17:13	8:38—9:13	9:26-36	
Lunatic boy healed	17:14-21	9:14-29	9:37-43	
Tax money from fish's mouth	17:24-27			
The parable of the wealthy farmer			12:16-21	
Crippled woman healed			13:10-13	
The parable of the lost sheep	18:12-13		15:3-7	
The parable of the lost coin			15:8-10	
The parable of the prodigal son			15:11-32	
The parable of the unmerciful servant	18:23-35			
Jesus and the rich young ruler	19:16—20:16	10:17-31	18:18-30	
The adulterous woman				8:1-11
Man born blind healed				9:1-41
The parable of the good shepherd				10:1-18
The parable of the good Samaritan			10:30-37	
The parable of the friend at midnight			11:5-10	

Chart Continued on Following Page

	MATTHEW	MARK	LUKE	JOHN
The parable of the good father			11:11–13	
Lazarus raised from the dead				11:1–44
Jesus heals ten lepers			17:11–19	
The parable of the laborers in the vineyard	20:1–16			
Jesus heals the blind men	20:29–34	10:46–52	18:35–43	
Jesus and the barren fig tree	21:18–22	11:12–14, 20–26		
The parable of the man with two sons	21:28–32			
Jesus and Zacchaeus			19:1–10	
The parable of the landowner	21:33–44	12:1–9	20:9–19	
The triumphal entry of Jesus	21:1–11	11:1–10	19:29–40	12:12–19
Jesus clears the temple	21:12–13	11:15–19	19:45–48	
The parable of the marriage feast	22:1–14		14:16–24	
The parable of the fig tree	24:32	13:28–31	21:29–33	
The parable of the virgins	25:1–13			
The parable of the man, his servants, and the talents	25:14–30			
Jesus looks ahead to His crucifixion	26:1–5	14:1–2	22:1–2	
Mary anoints Jesus	26:6–13	14:3–9		12:2–8
Judas plots with authorities	26:14–16	14:10–11	22:3–6	
Last Passover and the Lord's Supper	26:20–29	14:17–21	22:7–30	
Jesus in Gethsemane	26:36–46	14:32–42	22:39–46	18:1
Betrayal and arrest of Jesus	26:47–56	14:43–52	22:47–53	18:2–12
Jesus' trial before Caiaphas and the Sanhedrin	26:57–68	14:55–65	22:63–65	18:24
Peter denies Jesus	26:69–75	14:66–72	22:54–62	18:15–18
Jesus' trial before Pilate	27:11–26	15:1–15	23:1–25	18:28–40; 19:1–15
The crucifixion of Jesus	27:33–56	15:22–41	23:33–49	19:16–30
The burial of Jesus	27:57–61	15:42–47	23:50–56	19:38–42
The resurrection of Jesus	28:1–10	16:1–7	24:1–12	20:1–10
Post-resurrection appearances	28:9–10, 16–20	16:9–18	24:13–48	20:11–29; 21:1–22
The ascension of Jesus		16:19–20	24:50–53	

THE PALESTINE OF JESUS' TIME

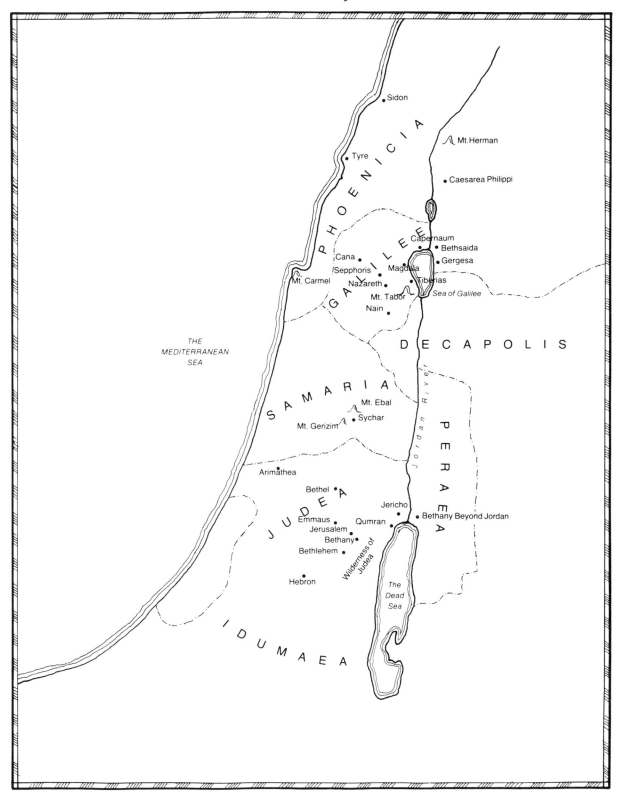

THE TRAVELS OF JESUS IN THE GOSPEL OF MATTHEW

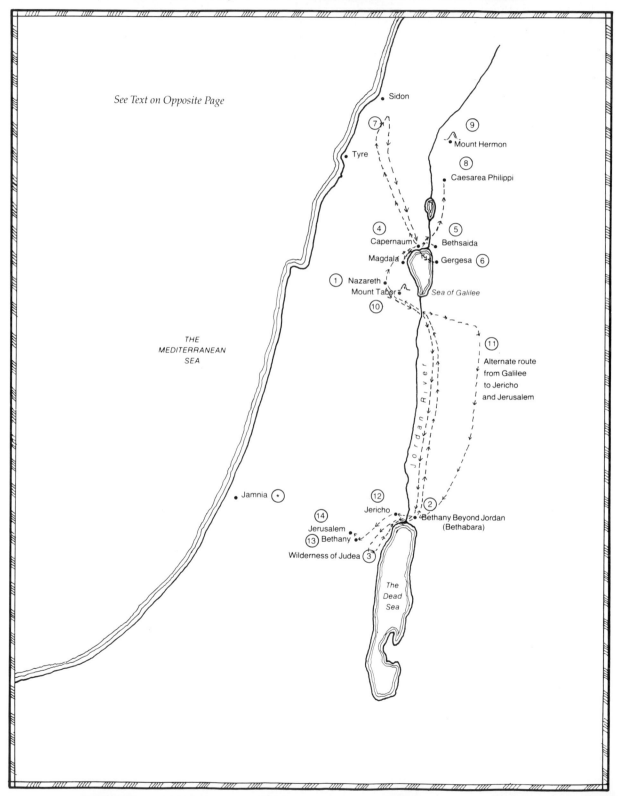

See Text on Opposite Page

Sidon

⑦

⑨

Mount Hermon

⑧

Tyre

Caesarea Philippi

④

⑤

Capernaum

Bethsaida

Magdala

Gergesa ⑥

① Nazareth

Mount Tabor

Sea of Galilee

⑩

THE
MEDITERRANEAN
SEA

⑪

Alternate route
from Galilee
to Jericho
and Jerusalem

J o r d a n   R i v e r

Jamnia ✱

⑫

②

Jericho

Bethany Beyond Jordan
(Bethabara)

⑭

Jerusalem

⑬ Bethany

Wilderness of Judea ③

*The
Dead
Sea*

Jesus leaves Nazareth ① and quite likely crosses the Jordan River a few miles below the Sea of Galilee and proceeds south on the east side of the river to Bethany beyond Jordan (Bethabara) ② where John the Baptist is preaching and baptizing. There, Jesus is baptized (Matt. 3:13–17).

Following Jesus' baptism He is led by the Spirit into the Wilderness of Judea ③ on the west side of the Dead Sea where He is tempted by Satan over a period of forty days (Matt. 4:1–11). Following the temptation experience it is quite likely that Jesus retraced His steps to Bethany beyond Jordan ② and then traveled north up the valley of the Jordan, forded the river, and returned to Nazareth ① (Matt. 4:12–13).

From Nazareth ① Jesus traveled north and east to Capernaum ④, modern Tell Hum, a fishing town on the north shore of the Sea of Galilee, where He apparently made His home. Capernaum ④ was a strategic location for Jesus to carry on much of His ministry since it was located on a much-traveled major highway.

Jesus then branched out and ministered throughout all of Galilee (Matt. 4:23–25), including Bethsaida ⑤ where He called Peter, Andrew, James, and John to be His disciples (Matt. 4:18–22).

Then we find Jesus and His disciples "went up into a mountain"—possibly just east of Capernaum ④, a few minutes' walk, where He delivered the Sermon on the Mount (Matt. 5–7). However, some authorities suggest that the "Sermon" was given in the *et Tabgha* area, located about two miles southwest of Capernaum. And others locate the "Sermon" site in a region known as the Horns of Hattin, south and a little west of Magdala.

From there Jesus returned to Capernaum ④ where He healed the centurion's servant and Peter's mother-in-law (Matt. 8:1–14). They next leave Capernaum ④ and cross the Sea of Galilee (where He calmed the storm) to the "country of the Gadarenes"—thought to be Gergesa ⑥ where He healed the two demoniacs (Matt. 8:23–34). They then returned to Capernaum ④ where Jesus continued His preaching and healing ministry, punctuated by one trip to Nazareth ① (Matt. 9:1, 13:58).

Matthew 14:13–21 gives us the story of the "Feeding of the 5,000"—the location is thought to be out from Bethsaida ⑤ "in a lonely place." Then from Capernaum Jesus traveled to the "region of Tyre and Sidon" ⑦ where He healed the Canaanite woman's daughter (Matt. 15:21–28) before returning to Capernaum ④.

From Capernaum ④ Jesus traveled almost thirty miles north to Caesarea Philippi ⑧ where Peter made his great profession of faith. From there Jesus "six days later" took Peter, James, and John to the mountain where He was transfigured—two sites are suggested: Mount Hermon ⑨, north of Caesarea Philippi ⑧ and Mount Tabor ⑩, located a short distance east of Nazareth ①. From there they returned to Capernaum ④.

Next, Jesus and His disciples moved south, probably by the Jordan Valley route to Judea (Matt. 19)—⑪ on the map traces an alternate route south which, because of its higher altitude, was frequently used in the heat of the summer as an option to the hot river route.

From there they moved west through Jericho ⑫ to Bethany ⑬ and Jerusalem ⑭ (Matt. 20:17). The remainder of Jesus' movements in Matthew occur in this vicinity.

While Jamnia ⊙ is not mentioned in the Gospels, it is referred to in the Matthew lesson material because of its importance to so much of what was happening in Judaism at the time of Matthew's writing. It was located in northern Judah just four miles inland from the Mediterranean Sea.

Following the destruction of Jerusalem in A.D. 70, the Jewish Sanhedrin met in Jamnia. It was here sometime between A.D. 92 and 100 that Jewish scholars met in an attempt to finalize their biblical Canon. This effort was precipitated by the controversy between Jews and Christians over which Hebrew writings should be included in the Canon.

JERUSALEM/JERICHO ENVIRONS

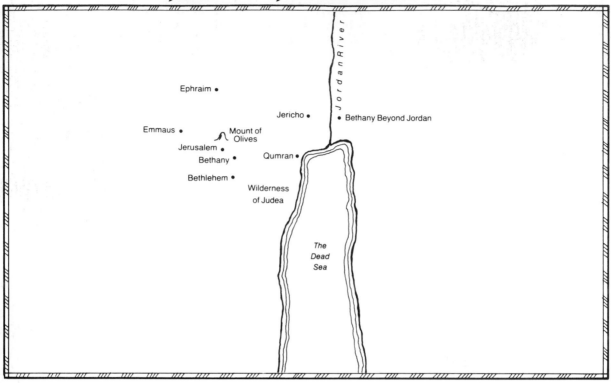

GALILEE

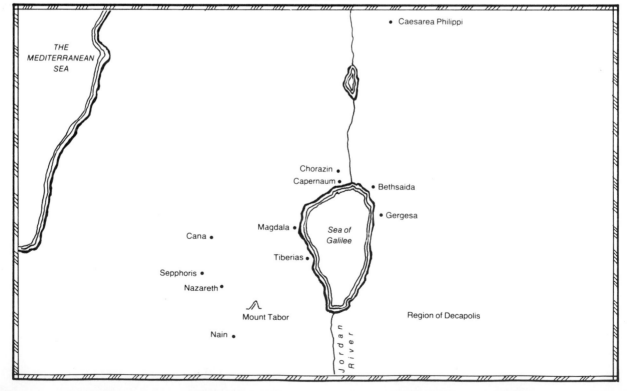